The
Agony
of the
Abuser

RON O

PAGE PUBLISHING, INC.
Conneaut Lake, PA

First originally published by Page Publishing 2021

ISBN 978-1-6624-2982-8 (pbk)
ISBN 978-1-6624-2983-5 (digital)

Printed in the United States of America

Domestic violence
Wife beaters
Fifty years of guilt
The mental pain and torment!
The fifty-year repentance!
It's hard to forgive myself!

INTRODUCTION

THIS BOOK IS about my early life as a domestic abuser; a wife beater who was deeply in love with his wife, but with a quick and violent temper; a person who drank every day and a person, when drinking, could not tolerate being challenged or criticized about anything. He could not walk away from a confrontation. He had to make you understand his point of view.

This is a revelation of the challenges with his personal demons. It is not based on any kind of clinical study. It is his personal story and quite real. It's true, I can only hope that someone else who has done similar things will read it and forgive themselves. This should apply to men and women because I have seen some women as mean, and I've seen men and women live their entire life fighting and abusing one another.

It's about how he spent the last fifty years suffering silently. It's about how he agonized with it and his effort to make up for what he had done. It's about a good and decent person who made some mistakes and couldn't forgive himself; about a person who has tried to treat everyone with respect and be thoughtful of their feelings and understanding of their mindset, the pressure on them, and what made them tick. He wanted to listen and understand her need to be heard, but it would end with him slapping her around. Although he has not hit a woman since 1972, it is still his bugaboo. The shame of letting people know that he beat his wife is unbearable, and the shame of revealing to people who know her what she was subjected to as a young woman weighed heavily on him.

I know that domestic violence is shameful, an act of cowardice, and there is no excuse for it. You always try to rationalize it that she made you do it. "If only she hadn't kept getting in my face when I told her to leave me alone, this would not have happened." You say to yourself, "Why does he stay here and go through this kind of life? He can find somebody who wouldn't make him mad." He thought about leaving many times but was scared because he felt that if he left, he would never come back.

CHAPTER ONE

Growing Up

I WAS BORN in 1944 into a family already with eight children, six boys and two girls. I was the seventh son and ninth child born in a family that would eventually grow to sixteen siblings. We were very poor, and I can recall them scrambling to have enough food for everyone to eat. There were times that we didn't have enough food too. I remember that the house we lived in had a lot of rooms but was straight and long. Looking back now, it seemed to be like a warehouse. I know we had some livestock, pigs, and chickens, and we would kill chickens for dinner. Where we lived was surrounded by farms, so we could glean the fields for vegetables.

My father worked, but I can't remember if his job was permeant or not. He worked construction, and in Delaware in the winter, I can't image any work being done, and I know that he didn't make a whole lot of money. I also know that they had a restaurant because I remember my mother teaching me how to make sub sandwiches and to wait on tables when I was nine years old. We were taught to be kind to people and that our job was more than waiting tables. It was to learn how to interact with the customers and see what we could learn from them. People always liked my mother, and some were very grateful to her because if they didn't have any money, she would run a tab for them. That has been a trait in my family; you could always go to any of my brothers' or sisters' home and eat. If you are family or neighbor, you could eat if you were hungry.

As I grew older, I couldn't see how poor we really were, but I also realized that many of those other people had it worse than we did. It was when I went into the Army, which was my first trip more than a few hundred miles from home, that I could see what the difference was between the rich and the really poor people. That's when I understood that I would be the best provider for my family and make sure my wife and kids were well cared for. I have reasonable expectations for what I needed to do. To be a good provider meant that I had to make the best out my experience in the Army.

We lived in this place called the Labor Camp. No, it wasn't forced living or anything like that. It looked like it could have been an old army barracks. It had a lot of houses outside the city limits, and I think everyone who lived in them were poor people with very large families. There was one family with twenty-two children and a lot with eight to twelve children, so we always had enough people to play with.

My childhood was filled with a lot of love because all my sisters and brothers were very sweet and respectful of each other. We played together and did a lot of things and looked out for each other, especially the younger ones. Even when we fought over something, we could never go to bed mad at each other. We all had to listen to what the older kids said, or we would get in trouble. We all went to Sunday school and church every week unless we were sick. Religion stuck with me throughout my life, even when I stopped going to church for a while. I would still pray every day. Sometimes I would pray several times a day. I just remembered that I was told that you never stop praying. I didn't know what that meant, but when I got depressed, I would read Psalm 51:1–3.

> "Have mercy upon me, O God, according to your lovingkindness: according unto the multitude of thy tender mercies blot out my transgressions. Wash me thoroughly from mine iniquity,

and cleanse me from my sin. For I acknowledge my transgressions: and my sin is ever before me."

Prayer always seemed to put my mind at ease. After praying, I would have a different thought pattern. The problem wasn't that urgent anymore. Sometimes I would know how to solve it, and other times I couldn't solve it, but it didn't weigh on me that much.

My mother died when I was twelve, and that was the first time that I experienced a great deal of grief in my life. I remembered that she went to the hospital to have a baby. The next thing they said, she was dead. Everybody was crying and sad, but I really couldn't understand what had happened because no one was really telling the younger children anything. I asked my oldest sister, Rebecca, about it, and all she did was hug me real tight and said, "I'm the mother now." I wasn't crying because I saw everybody else crying, and I wanted to help them or stop them. I didn't know what to do, but I didn't cry.

It was Tuesday, April 9, 1957, when she died. For some reason, I always remembered that day when the news came. I was standing in this large room at the end of the house. It was the dining room where they would sell their food. It was my uncle who brought it to my father. He was at the hospital when she passed away. Uncle Simon was always around us. He was very close to his sister. Uncle Simon and my father were crying, and I was watching them, but not crying.

She was to be buried on April 13, which was a Saturday. The day before the funeral, Rebecca told me that we wouldn't see mother anymore and that she would be the sister and the mother. I recall her saying that "I haven't seen you crying yet, so let's have a good cry. It will help you remember Mother the way she was." She hugged me and said, "It's okay to let people see you crying." She said that Mother will see us crying, and she would ask God to comfort us. Then she said, "You will always miss Mother because you love her and she loves you. When you think about her, be happy that she sees us." I still see my brothers and sisters on that April day as they heard about her death; they all had the same type of reaction: sadness, a lot of grief, and painful feelings.

Rebecca took over the duties as head of the household, and we all loved her and followed the rules that she set for us. Rebecca was only twenty-two when Mother died, and she had a child of her own as well as a stepson. But she did everything that she could to see that we were provided for. Life was tough for us, but we all had discipline in ourselves and respect for others. Rebecca lived with her husband and kids, so she as not with us every day but always there when we needed her.

My father was there too. He would cook breakfast for us and get us ready for school. He hired a woman to help around the house in the afternoon so that someone would be at home when we got there. Still he did most of the cooking and other chores that needed to be done. We also had chores assigned to us to be done after school. Daddy was really having a hard time dealing with my mother's death, but I don't know if anyone else noticed it. He was very quiet and withdrawn most of the time. I would see him crying sometimes when he thought he was alone. Daddy did the best he could after we lost Mother, but I could feel the loneliness in him. He was a good storyteller. He would tell us ghost stories and get us scared to be in the dark.

I remember he told us a story about this man riding a horse around the lake every night, trying to find something he had lost. Only one person in the whole town knew what he was looking for until one day he (Daddy) waited to see the man on the horse. That night Daddy was hiding in a tree, and here came the man on the horse, looking for something that he had lost. My father said the reason he couldn't find what he was looking for was because the man lost his head and couldn't find it because he didn't have any eyes, so he wouldn't see it anyway. We were afraid to go past Silver Lake at night for fear that we would see the headless rider or some other kind of monster that he told us about.

The next three or four months were a little rough because I was always helping Mother in the kitchen, making sandwiches or clearing tables or some other chore. Now there was nothing to do, and Daddy was still out, trying to do the work he was doing. A lot the time I was doing my homework, but that never took me too long to

get done. The few chores that were assigned to me were not too difficult or time-consuming, so I had a lot of time on my hands. Most of
the time the only person there for me to talk to was the housekeeper,
and she would be hugging me a lot, telling me how sweet I was.

When I was approaching thirteen, the housekeeper told me that
she had a good birthday present for me. But she had to show me
some things first so that the present would be good for me. She said
that this had to be our secret, and I couldn't tell anybody about it
because then she couldn't give me the present. I said, "Okay, I promise not to tell." At that point, she unzipped my pants, put her hand
on my penis, and started massaging it. She kept asking me if it felt
good. Of course, it did. I said, "Yeah." That was the first time that I
had seen anything come out before. I didn't know what happened.

I was the first one home from school every day, about two hours
before the other children. Two days went by, and the housekeeper
called me to her room and said that she was going to show me something else and that this was part of what I was going to get on my
birthday when I got the real present. This time she unbuttoned my
pants and pulled my underwear down and performed oral sex on me.
I didn't tell anybody about it, and I didn't know what was going on,
but I liked it and did what she told me. She said, "One more week
for the big surprise. Make sure you don't tell, or I can't give it to you."

My birthday is November 24, but before my birthday, she told
me that I was going to get my present early because everybody would
be home on the weekend. Near the end of the week, she told me to
come home from school early because she was giving it to me that
day, and she would write a note to the teacher, telling him that I had
to go to the doctor. I was excited about getting the present. I never
thought about what it would be. I just wanted to see what it was.

It was the Friday before my birthday when I came home and
went to her room. She told me, "Don't be scared. I will show you
what to do." She took her clothes off and put my hand on her breast
and said, "Just massage them easy with your fingers." While I was
doing that, she pulled my pants down and lay back on the bed while
pulling me on top of her. She was kissing me and massaging my penis

11

at the same time. She then put me inside her and said, "When I push up, you push down and just keep on pushing."

She was about thirty-five years old, and I was going to be thirteen in a couple days. It was the first time that I had sex, and even though I liked it, something felt weird about it. After we finished, she washed me with soap and water and said, "Always clean yourself up after you do it with a woman." I was still waiting for the present, and she noticed that I was looking around for it and said, "I want to be the first person to give you $50 to spend for anything you want. Today was a special present, but I will give you the other one on your birthday." She gave me $50 on my birthday and whispered, "Thanks for letting me give you the special present too." We continued having secret sex encounters for about four or five months until one day she told me that we couldn't do it in the house anymore. Something strange happened to me about a month after my birthday, and I didn't realize for forty years what it was.

My father, who never whipped me and always had a great deal of patience with me, suddenly seemed to not want me around. I didn't do anything, and he never told me what was wrong; our relationship just changed. My afterschool chore was to fill the wood box (we still had woodburning stoves) and the coal bend so that there would be enough to keep the fire burning through the night. I was obedient and did what I was told, so I seldom got into trouble. However, I would ask questions about why things had to be a certain way.

I had dropped some wood in the box crooked and started to get another load. Daddy said to put that wood in the box straight. I said I would when I brought in the last load. Before I knew it, he had picked up a piece of the wood and hit me in the head. I fell to the floor and got up and started to say something, and he said, "Do what I say." About ten minutes later, my head was bleeding, and he took me to the sink and worked on it until it stopped. He didn't say anything, but I could see in his face that he wanted to tell me that he was sorry, but he seemed to be in shock. I didn't tell any of my brothers or sisters because I had no idea what I had done. A couple days went by, and I had a bad headache, and Daddy took me to the doctor (they didn't ask questions in those says). He left me at my aunt Estella's house while he did some errands.

Aunt Estella was my mother's sister, and we lived just a few miles apart. While I was there, she asked me how things were at home, and I told her they were fine. She said, "What did you go to the doctor for?" "It was because I have a bad headache, and it won't stop," I said. Aunt Estella had about six or seven children close to my age, and her husband (Uncle John) had a high-paying job. They were in much-better financial condition than we were. As she asked me questions about home, I had a hard time answering them. She must have sensed something was wrong because she asked me if I wanted to come and live with her. I told her yes, and she said, "I will tell Henry (my father) that I want you to live with us." When he came to pick me up, they talked. At first, he was shaking his head; but after a while, he said, "All right."

We went home and got my clothes, and from that point on, I stayed with Aunt Estella and her family. They never did anything or say something to make me uncomfortable, but because of things the kids said and did, I felt out of place. My cousin would say, "You should wait until the family finish eating before you eat." I would be sitting, watching them eat, and my aunt would say, "What are you waiting for? Get over here and eat your dinner." Aunt Stella (that's what we called her) was one of those people who seemed to understand everything. She would have a serious conversation with you and talk about any problem she thought you might have, and you didn't even know how she knew about it.

Another time my cousins knew I was afraid of rats, so one morning I woke up, and there was a big rat lying on my chest. It scared me so bad I wet my pants. I told Aunt Stella what they did, and she said, "If you let them get away with it, they will keep on teasing you." I said, "What do I do about it?" She said I would know when it's time to stop the crying and being scared every day. I knew that my cousins liked me. I was just the new toy in the shed, and they liked to play with me. Nevertheless, I had to figure a way to join them with the pranks, and maybe they would leave me alone.

One day we were climbing this big tree that hung over the house. I told my cousin that I was going to climb to the top and jump off the roof. He was two years older than me and knew that I would really hurt myself if I jumped. He said, "You will kill yourself if you jump from there." He was scared that I was serious and kept talking to me, trying to keep me from jumping. Then he said, "I'm not playing with you anymore because you can't take a joke." I honestly had not thought about suicide. I thought that I was playing prank on him, but he thought that I was contemplating suicide. When I came down, he said, "I was scared that you were going to jump or fall." I said that I was just teasing him like he did me; I wasn't going to jump. He said, "No more jokes like that because somebody could get hurt." Then I knew what she meant. Without knowing it, I had changed the way my cousins reacted with me. It was like they now accepted me—no strings attached.

I felt much better about living with them after that, and even though there were things that bothered me, I could take the remarks that I couldn't take before. I was still withdrawn and spent a lot of time alone. Life became more fun, and when I wanted to join them in anything, I did. Aunt Stella liked politics, so I would talk to her a lot about current events. We would sit and read the newspaper and watch the TV. She taught me a lot about knowing the person you want to vote for. She said, "Read about them, find everything you can about them. Don't just vote because somebody else likes them. Make your vote count for something."

I lived close to my father, and Aunt Stella made sure that I went to see him at least three days a week. She would always tell me that my father loves me and that he was having a hard time dealing with my mother's death. She said, "Always respect your father and your family because no one will ever love you the way they do." I remember learning so many things from her. She made me feel important from the first day she asked me to stay with them. I feel now that she must have sensed that there was a problem with me and Daddy.

I went home to see my family often. Daddy would pick me up anytime. She didn't care when, just that I or he told her that he was picking me up and when he was bringing me back. Daddy never mentioned hitting me with that log, but I could tell he regretted it. He would be hugging me and rubbing my hands with his special liniment. When I went for a visit, it was as if I hadn't left. We did nothing special, just like before, playing games, bullying each other.

I would always see the housekeeper when we drove up but never saw her except for dinner, and then she disappeared. At that age, my thoughts were far away from her. Of course, I thought about the sex, but that was something that I never asked for or even knew how to ask for it. And I didn't even think about any of it seriously until I was an adult. I was about thirty-five years old before I knew that I had been molested as a child. That is still a secret that I am revealing now for the first time publicly.

I lived with Aunt Stella until I was sixteen, and then I moved to my sister Rebecca's house about twenty-five miles away. She was going to pay me to help watch her children while they were at work. I went to school, and since I had already completed most of the required courses, I only went for three classes and was back home. When the kids came home, I would give them a snack and put them down for a nap. Then I would clean up around the house and sometimes cook dinner. When she got home, it was done. He was a truck driver and would be gone the whole week and come back on the weekend.

Her husband, Bummy, was a quiet man who drank way too much, but he was determined to support his family and therefore never missed any time off work. I loved him also because even though he didn't want to do it, he still allowed her take us in if we needed help. He would call me a parasite when he didn't like something that I was doing, then a couple of hours later, he'd say, "You know I didn't mean that. You're a good man."

CHAPTER TWO

Young Adult

DURING THE TIME that I stayed with Rebecca, I had developed a good work habit. I knew what I had to do, so I got it done quickly. The first real job outside the house was for a construction company pouring blacktop in the summer. It was hot, and the sun was hot. I probably weighed 130 pounds and losing more every second, but I knew what I had to do, so I did my best to get it done. For a whole week, I showed up every day and did what I was told. Then Friday came; it was payday, and he gave everybody a check but the four high school kids. We asked about our check, and he said that we must work a week and then get paid after the second week. We waited for the next payroll and didn't get paid. He told us that we would start getting paid next week, and we would be getting paid for two weeks, and the company would still owe us for one week.

When we went to work on Monday morning, no one was there. We waited until about nine o'clock and went and asked the property owner if we could call the contractor, and he said, "What are you kids hanging around here for?" We said that we came to work on the road. We had been helping for three weeks. He said that they finished the job last week, and they were not coming back there anymore. We were mad because we knew that we wouldn't be getting paid, that we spent three weeks working for nothing. How could anyone treat us like that? We were trying to make an honest buck, and he stole it from us.

We wanted to go and get the money, but since he picked us up on the corner (that's where you would stand in the morning and people who needed help would pick you for the day or whatever they needed), we didn't know how to find him. We didn't even know the guy's name. Three weeks of hard work, and nothing to show for it. We looked for those trucks for months but never could find a trace of that crook. I'm glad because we might have done something terrible to him.

That was my first encounter with a real job that wasn't for a relative. At sixteen I was just happy to say I got a job. The next time I got a job, I made sure that I knew who they were and where their office was located. I learned how to ask about the pay before I took a job. Bummy told me, "Don't be so anxious to go to work that you don't know how much you are being paid." That is another thing that has haunted me for many years: how could a grownup do this to kids who just want to work and make some honest money?

My next encounter with an employer was better because it was at a company that made bricks and cinder blocks. It was the company that my brother-in-law, Bummy, worked for. I was still very inexperienced at working on my own but always willing to learn and do a great job. Given the chance, I knew that I could do anything put before me. And with my brother-in-law being a senior employee, they wouldn't bother me too much.

The first couple days they showed me how to separate the good blocks from those with cracks or some other deformity, such as blocks that were not even or had bubbles or were not the correct size. I had to stack them on pallets and send them to be crushed. If some good blocks were in the pile, then they were to be put on a pallet and returned to the shipping area. There were as many good blocks in the pile as were bad ones. This work was harder than working on the road because I had to touch every block in the pile, good or bad. I was just in an area away from there other workers and hardly had any contact with them other than breaks and lunch.

I was a quick learner, and it didn't take too long before I was given more responsibility around the yard (i.e., driving the forklift and loading the truck with the cement pipe). The boss and owner also employed my sister on a part-time basis to watch their children and do special parties, etc. He would bring me home from work because he lived just a few blocks away from us. He would always eat at our house; maybe that's why he always wanted to bring me home. He would drive me home, but if I couldn't get somebody to give me a ride, I'd have to walk to work in the morning. It was three miles from the city limits of Dover to the city limits of Camden; you can add another half mile to the plant. Sometimes I could catch a ride with our neighbor, but much of the time I walked. I would hitchhike but hardly ever got a ride because much of the time it would be early in the morning and still near darkness. Truth be told, I was as scared to take a ride as they were to give me a ride.

Having some uncertainty getting to work in the morning caused some problems; though I was mostly on time, there were still some times when I showed up late. Those were usually days that I had to walk all the way from home, about three and a half miles. By the time I got to work, I was too tired to perform the way I did when I had a regular ride. The neighbor had gotten hurt on his job, so I couldn't catch a ride with him anymore. I had to be to work at six in the morning, so I had to leave home at three thirty or four in the morning to get there on time. And if I was lucky enough to hitch a ride and get there early, I still couldn't stat work until six. There were times I had to sit there and wait two hours before I could get started.

Even at seventeen years old I could read the writing on the wall. I knew that I wasn't the great worker as when I started because I know that my production was not what it was. I knew that sooner or later I would be fired if I didn't do better. I had to find a way to improve my late arrivals, or I would lose the job. I can't remember exactly, but I think that I was making around one dollar and seventy-five cents ($1.75) an hour, fourteen dollars ($14.00) a day, or ninety dollars ($90.00) a week. That was okay money for a seventeen-year-old. I didn't know what to do about it, but every time I got to work late, I thought would be the last day. My brother-in-law was feeling the pressure too because I wouldn't have the job if he didn't work there. I know that because the foreman reminded me on every occasion that he was the reason that I got the job and that I was making him look bad. Finally, the word came down that I was no longer needed and that Friday would be my last day. I was devastated but not surprised because I had recognized the problem but did not know how to solve it. I was sadder that my brother-in-law would suffer for me not being to work like I should be.

About a week later, he was laid off too. I was fired. He was laid off, which meant that he still had a job; he just wasn't working for a while. I told him that I really tried to be on time, and it was tough when I had to walk all the way then stack brick all day. I was just too weak to keep up the pace. He said that "some grown men had more of a problem keeping up with production than you did." I told him that I was sorry that he lost his job because of me. He said that the plant closes for two weeks every year and that he would be back at work. The layoff had nothing to do with me. I was relieved that I didn't cause him to lose his job. I was still fired, though, and had to find another job.

My next job was working as a salesman, selling sewing machines. This guy was recruiting people to sell Singer sewing machines. When you sold a machine, you would receive a commission. I don't remember how much, but it was more than a week's pay at the brickyard. I signed up with him (it was about ten people who signed up), and he trained us for about a week then took us on our first appointment. He was going to show us how, what he taught us worked in the field. We had to make the appointment, and then he would go with us to demonstrate the sewing machine. He taught us how to tread it and unclog it when it got too much tread in the feed thing.

I asked an old guy who was kind of a mentor to me who I would ask. He gave me a list of older people who had a need for sewing machine. I never thought about asking these people before he told me. Hank was his name, and he was maybe sixteen or seventeen years older than me, but he liked me because he thought that I was smart and needed an older person for guidance. Hank would never tell you anything without quizzing you about it before you left his presence.

He would say repeat what I said, then we were finished. He said that this way, he would know if he told me something wrong.

I did what he said. I asked people who owned cleaners and tailors and women who made dresses. I got a dozen appointments in three weeks and sold nine Singer sewing machines. He kept telling me, "You are my top salesman. Keep up the good work." I wasn't the only one doing good because he had a white board with the sales listed, and there were seven of us who had sold more than four machines. In that group were adults as well as, I think, three teenagers. It was new to us that you could make so much money selling stuff like this.

We all were looking forward to a big payday when the checks came from headquarters. It was delayed a couple of times, but we were assured that they would be there. On Friday afternoon we all gathered at the office to get paid for our sales, which the boss said was the best group sales in the whole country. The crew was all there, the adults and the teenagers, waiting to see who made the most money and who would receive biggest bonus. Those with a lot of sales were kind of heroes. The others wanted to know how you made the appointments or where you found people. I think everyone was genuinely happy for the other people; they seemed happy to be a part of the group.

We waited as the afternoon got closer to evening, and the boss had not shown up with the checks. Some of the older people began to get worried about him. They thought that he should have been there by now. One secretary who worked in the office called headquarters and was told that there were no checks due because each invoice was paid when they came in and that he had been paid for a substantial number of machines in the past two months. Another person scheming to take advantage of people. Another time that I put a lot of effort into something that was a fraud from the beginning. All I could think about the boss and his training tactic of when they open the door, put your foot in so that they must listen. He said that they will not close the door if your foot is in the way. And though I never did that, I really wanted to put my foot somewhere if we could ever see him again.

Just before I turned eighteen, I got a job at the cold storage, which was right behind our house, about three hundred feet to work. I knew that this job was temporary because they hired me because of the upcoming holiday season. They handled frozen food storage for several companies. They froze everything, but mostly poultry, turkeys, chickens, geese, and duck, etc. So my job was to load the trucks when the crew bought the items from the freezer, put it on the dock, then we put it on the truck.

The job was to last until January, and it would be part-time because I was under eighteen, so they could only work me I think it was twenty-five hours a week. I would be eighteen in a couple of months, and shortly after that, the job would be ending anyway. Since I lived so close, if somebody was going to miss work, they would send someone to my house and tell that I was needed that day or night. I normally worked as much as the full-time employees, and no one ever said anything, and I got paid too. I have always been the person to look at how I could do the job more efficiently and was not afraid to say that if we did it this way that we could get more done. They would call me in all the time when people were sick with colds mostly, but for other reasons too.

After I was on the job for about two months, we were four guys short, and we had seven trucks at the dock to be loaded for outbound delivery. There we four trucks in line to be unloaded. There were six people in the freezer and six loading trucks; two men per truck. We were falling behind, and I suggested that we put one man loading a truck, have the guys in the freezer drop the product in the freezer, and the ones loading the trucks go into the freezer and pick up their orders. At first the boss said no, but the next day, before we started work, they would go over things before we started work. He said that he had thought about what I said and wanted to give it a try. The men in the freezer were happy and so were the loaders. Because of Hank—I talked about him as my mentor earlier—who had been working there for about twenty years, the men liked me. If Hank was your friend, you got some respect because Hank commanded so much respect from many people on many levels.

The boss even talked to me about my idea in front of the workers. I explained that there was a lot of the dock not being used; it just had trucks sitting there. We tried it, and the day just happened to be a little less busy than normal, so we weren't rushed to get things done. The experiment worked pretty well. The freezer guys who rotated out were happy, so we knew that we needed to rotate the men every couple hours. After about three weeks, we had virtually adopted that method of operation. Loading the trucks quicker made for less stress because we were always behind, and the drivers had to wait three or four hours sometime. It didn't cause anybody to lose their job because we were that busy. Drivers still had to wait one or two hours. I gained a lot of respect from the crew.

I was eighteen now and full-time. I could work as much overtime as I wanted, and I did every chance I got. Just before Christmas, the night supervisor was going to leave the company—I don't know why. But they were looking for a new supervisor, and the boss came to me and told me that the crew had asked him to make me the new supervisor. "What do you think?" he asked. I said that I didn't know if I could be a supervisor. He said, "Before you tell me anything, talk to Hank." I called Hank and he said that he would talk to me before work. When I got there, all the crew was there, and they said that they would show me what I needed to know. They wanted me to take the job as their supervisor because they didn't want somebody new coming from outside.

Hank convinced me that it would be a good move and more money ($750 a month in 1962). I took the job and did well. The crew never gave me any problems. I knew how to do a lot of the paperwork already, so that wasn't a problem either. I would ask a crew member, "Do you want to load this truck?" They always said yes, but Hank told me, "You're the boss. Don't ask them if they want to do it. Tell them to do it. What are you going to do if they say, 'No, I don't want to do it'? Tell them, 'I need you to load this truck,' and give them the order and say, 'Thanks, I appreciate your help.'" He also said, "When they finish, tell them that you have another load for them, but say, 'You guys take a little break and warm up some.'" They loved the fact that I wasn't bossy and showed them respect.

After all, every one of the crew was at least eight years older than me. I worked there until I was twenty and told them that I was applying for a job at the new General Foods plant opening down the street. This would be a higher-paying job, and it was another mile away from my house.

CHAPTER THREE

Manhood

WHILE I WAS working at the cold storage, I met the beautiful woman in the city of Dover. My sister was also a part-time beautician. She would do women's hair in her kitchen to make extra money. She would have three or four women waiting in line on the weekend. I would help her some time by doing the shampoo while she was curling or whatever she had. I liked hanging around the women; although I was shy and wouldn't talk to them much. Rebecca would tell some of them, "He can't wait to wash your hair, he's got a crush on you." That wasn't true. I wanted to talk to them but was afraid that I might get my feelings hurt if I said the wrong thing.

This one day I was sitting there, waiting to wash someone's hair. Across the street, I saw this girl at a friend's house just standing there, very beautiful and very shapely. The perfect body, I had to find a way to talk to her. I knew her cousin but had never seen her. I went across the street and said, "Alice [her cousin], do you want anything from the store?" It was hot that day, and Alice said, "Bring me a coke." Then I asked her if she wanted anything, but she said no. I said, "It's hot today. You need something to cool you down," but she said no again. I said, "Well, can you come a help me carry them back?" She didn't say anything. I said, "If you go with me, you will need something to drink." Alice told her to go with me, and she did. Turned out that she knew all my sisters and brothers in Dover. I had been there for a couple of years, and I never saw her, but she said that she had seen me a lot of times.

When she walked to the store with me, I found the words to ask her to go to the movies with me, and she said yes. She was eighteen and didn't have a boyfriend and never had one. I don't know why I had not seen her before; she lived only a few blocks from me. I said to her, "Why haven't I seen you before? You live so close, and your cousin lives right across the street from me." Because I had found some nerves from somewhere, I wanted to stay on a roll. I had a lot of questions and asked her everything that came to my mind.

I talked all the way to the store and back. Just before we got back, she told me that she saw me with these married women. I said, "Where do you see me?" She told me that she saw me going in the woman's house after her husband leaves for work. That was true, but I denied that there was anything going on. I said we were just friends. She said, "I saw you kissing her through the window in the alley." I was caught in a lie, but I told her, "I used to go with her, but now she just teases me." She knew that this woman was older than me and that it scared her because she had never even kissed a boy, and I had an older woman.

I don't want to use the name of the married woman, so I will call her Billie. She was four years older and was married to a man twenty-five years older than she was. She married him so that she could help her struggling mother. We never went anywhere or did anything but have sex. She was never going to leave her husband for any reason because he had a good job and made a lot of money, plus I think she loved him; she just likes sex more. Sometimes we would go at it all day. Now I've met Mae, a person more my age, and now that I think about it, I had never been with a woman who was not more than four years older. It was always one of my sister's friends or an older woman who I met on my own.

Billie had already told me that she didn't want me to come around anymore, so that wouldn't be a problem. Now I needed to know how to keep Mae interested in me. We were going to the movies later that day. I didn't know what to say. I knew that I wanted to be with her. I wanted her to be my girlfriend. She was receptive of me, and I was moving slow, trying not to come off too cocky. I wanted her to like me because if my feelings got hurt, I knew that I wouldn't talk to her anymore out of fear.

This was the first time in my life that I ever approached a girl, and it was nerve-racking to me. I think that I had her attention after we went to the store. By the time we got back, she was talking about herself a lot, how she had never been kissed and she wanted a man who was honest and where she wanted to be when she had the first kiss. She said that she would not have her first kiss on the back seat of a car nor would she go with a man unless she loved him. I asked her how long it would take before she knew that she loved a man. She said, "I know now, so it doesn't take long." That went over my head, and I missed it. When I realized what she had said, I thought, what a dummy, she was telling me that she liked me.

I was almost twenty years old and knew that I might be drafted in the coming months. In my state, it was certain that when you turned twenty and a half, you would be getting your notice. For some reason, the draft ended, and the papers didn't come. The recruiter told me that I would still be getting called as soon as I turned twenty and a half and that it might be better if I sign up voluntarily; that way, I could get the kind of job I wanted. I talked to my brothers because they had spent their time and thought it was great.

Mae and I were learning a lot about each other, and we seemed to enjoy being together. We both preferred being alone, so we would go to the park or a walk around town, but mostly we kept to ourselves. I was so happy that I had found someone on my own, and nobody demanded any of our time. We did whatever we wanted to when we wanted to, and people didn't bother to care because we were doing what we choose.

Opportunities started becoming available for me. There was a new processing plant coming to the city and was hiring several hundred people. Because it was a national operation, everybody wanted to work for them, and your chances of getting the job were great. I had experience working in the shipping department, and that was a dire need for them. I put in my application and was hired to work in the shipping and receiving department. However, the plant would not be operational for a few months. I still gave my notice to the cold storage because they needed to replace me. The excitement grew as I waited for the new job to come on line. It wasn't stressful because I was working every day, and the job had been assigned to me. I had been hired. We were just waiting for our notice when we would start work.

Mae and I had been together about six months now and were talking about being married. She had also gotten a job, and we only saw each other a few hours a day because my shift at the cold storage was from two thirty in the afternoon to ten thirty at night. She worked from eight a.m. to four thirty p.m. We had lunch together. I would meet her for lunch, and she would meet me for dinner around seven p.m.

I got the call for my new job and was to start in two weeks. But that two weeks turned into four weeks because of problems they had with inspections. I told them at the cold storage, and they let me stay on for two more weeks. I finally went to work for my new employer and was there for three weeks before the recruiter told me that I had to report for active duty.

The war in Vietnam was heating up, and the draft was coming back, and I would be in the first group since I was almost twenty and a half. He said, "You can pick the job you want if you enlist for another year." Since my brothers thought it was a good move for me when the draft was in effect, I enlisted for the extra year. Off I would go to the Army for the next three years and maybe more if I liked it. It was several years later that I learned the recruiter was lying to boost his recruitment stats. He made us think that we were still going to be drafted because of the war. The draft had ended in 1964, and we had no obligation to enlist.

CHAPTER FOUR

On My Own

I THOUGHT IT was the best thing to happen in my life thus far, and though I was working, I suddenly did not feel good about my circumstances. Being drafted was an opportunity for me because I had a chance to make something of myself, do some traveling, and see how other people in the world lived. At the urging of my older brothers, instead of going in through the draft, I went down and enlisted for a three-year tour so that I could have a chance to pick what I wanted to do; it also gave me time to adjust to the fact that I would be really on my own.

I was promised that I would be placed in an administration position once we finished basic training. That didn't happen. For a while the disappointment started to envelop me because I thought that I had been lied to, to have me sign up for the extra year. I figured that if they would start with a lie, then everything else would be even worse as time passed. I knew that I had no choice now but to report to my assigned duty station, or I could be put in jail for disobeying an order. I did report for basic training at Fort Jackson South Carolina on March 8, 1965.

I was quickly overwhelmed with the way the operation worked. After all this, I still thought it was best thing to happen in my life thus far; and though I was working, I did not feel good about my circumstances. Some of the men hated that I talked too much and caused problems for everyone else. At first, I didn't see that happening, but I soon found out that if I asked why a certain thing was done, it would soon be a project for everybody. An example: I was always awake a couple hours before the wakeup call, so I asked the drill sergeant for permission to do the monkey bars before breakfast just to get in some extra work. The next thing I heard was the sergeant telling everybody that I wanted to do the monkey bars before breakfast, so everybody had to report at four thirty to do the exercise. Of course, they all blamed me of having to get up earlier to exercise, and some even threatened me if I opened my mouth again.

There was one thing that I didn't like about basic training, and that's the mail formations. They would call all these people out for mail call, and you had to stand there and wait for them to call your name. Many guys never got a single postcard the whole time they were in training. To me it was sad to see them waiting to hear their name and never did. One guy, his name was the same as mine, would write two letters every day but didn't get one in the ten weeks we were in basic.

The one thing that made me popular in basic training was the letters that I received from my girlfriend. Every day at mail call I would receive letters from my girl, and my good friend, Alice, would write me every day too. There were soldiers there who never got any mail, so sometimes I would let them read some of mine. My girlfriend would write me letters on big sheets of paper, I mean two feet by two feet wide, and they smelled good too. Alice, my best friend, would write very beautiful letters. I shared hers the most; she really knew how to make you feel good. Those letters also made being away from home much easier. Just knowing that you had someone there missing you as much as you missed them was truly comforting. I know that my family missed me too. I was everybody's favorite brother.

To hear from my girlfriend every day, telling me how much she loved me and couldn't wait for me to come home, really put some pep in my steps. I was the happiest recruit at Fort Jackson South Carolina; that's where I spent my first ten weeks of military duty. I didn't care where I trained. I just wanted to be the best soldier so that

I could get my leave on time. That was my whole motivation to complete every course on time, and I did. For ten weeks, we marched and ran (I could really run in those days), did field exercises, etc. I loved it all. There was this section where we trained, they called it "drag-ass hill." If I can remember, it was an uphill run that went on an upgrade for eight miles. I don't know if that's true, but it was a long run up, and that's what they used to tell us.

I've always been obedient to anyone one in charge of me. Whatever I was told to do, I did it if it was legal. I rarely had any questions about the work that I was assigned and completed every task the best I could. If I were assigned KP duty, I did it with a smile, or mopping floors—no problem. Any physical activity came easy for me. However, I could not crack eggs fast enough. I would crack them one at a time because I could stand the shell being in the pot. When I saw a piece of the shell, I had to get it out, so I was very careful trying not to get shells in the eggs.

There was this really short drill sergeant. Thomas was his name. Well, he asked me why I was smiling during our morning exercises (I always had a smile on my face. I never heard anyone complain about it. The fact is, everyone would tell me that smiling made life more pleasant, but he was also the drill sergeant.) I said, "No reason, Sergeant." That was a mistake. He told me that there was a reason, and I would do push-ups until I told him what it was. As I was doing the push-ups, I was trying to think of a good reason to give him. After about three hundred push-ups, he asked me again, "Why are you smiling when everyone else is not?" I said, "I'm happy, sir. I'm always happy, sir." He didn't know what to say, but from that time forward, he liked me and let it be known to the others.

He would watch me, though, and every time I made any kind of mistake or blunder, he would be all over me. He'd make me run up and down the steps with my footlocker on my shoulder or run until he got tired. But he would make the other people do it too, and some of them hated me. There was a time when we were on the shooting range, and I had to qualify with the .45 caliber handgun, and I was lousy. I could not hit the broad side of a barn with that gun. The M14 rifle I was an expert. I hit the bull's-eye nine out of ten times. The sergeant would be yelling and screaming at me about not qualifying with the .45. While we were on the range, he was yelling at me, and I looked at him. You could see the fear on his face. He suddenly stopped screaming at me, and the rest of the training he worked with me showing me how to shot the .45. Later he was talking to me and told me that he thought I was going to shoot him. (I had no thoughts of shooting anybody.) I said, "Why would you think that?" He said, "When I was screaming at you, I saw death in your eyes. I thought that I had pushed you too far." I said, "No, I am not shooting anybody."

The time for graduations was near, and I had passed all my training and was assured that I would be going home for three weeks. At last I would be able to see my brothers and sisters—I know they missed me—and Alice to thank her for all the letters that she had sent to me. Most of all, I couldn't wait to see my girlfriend because from the letters that she had written, I knew that I wanted to marry her more than anything. Even though Mae and I were engaged, I guess that I really started loving her once I was away from home. Those letters were very thoughtful and really made me feel that she loved me and couldn't wait until we were together again. They always had a wonderful smell and sometimes kissing lips on them. Everybody noticed them and made comments about them. Then I got this letter from Mae; I think it was two feet by two feet wide. That's when this one soldier from Philadelphia whom I had befriended (his name was also Ronald) asked if he could read some of my letters (he hadn't received one letter the whole time we were there). I let him read it and another soldier, and then another wanted to read my good-smelling letters, and I enjoyed letting them read them too. They were clean, no profanity or sexual stuff, just saying how much she loved me and current events at home.

Several weeks went by, and we were nearing the seventh week of training, and I was looking forward to mail call; but to my surprise, I only got a letter from Alice. The whole time that I was in the Army, her letters came three times a week. We could use the telephone after our shift and on the weekend to call home. Her mother didn't have a telephone, so I had to call my sister and have her to tell Mae that I was going to call her. Since we had to wait in line to get the phone, she had to wait forever for the call, and man, was she happy when we talked but said that she had been sick and didn't feel up to writing. She put so much thought into every letter that I could understand that; so she did write me a couple letters a day, but the excitement seemed to be dwindling, but it was later when I realized that.

The time had come, and I was finally going home for three weeks before I had to report to Fort Sill, Oklahoma, for my advanced training. Mae and I were spending a lot of time together, and our plan to get married was looking good. She acted like I was the best thing that ever happened to her. Mae was only nineteen years old, and I was almost twenty-one, but we both were levelheaded people who seemed to know what we wanted. Those days to that point were the best days of my life. I was walking around town in my uniform, and she was always by my side. People knew my sisters and brothers and always thought that I was a nice, young man (I never got into any trouble) and that I showed a lot of respect for them. Those three weeks went fast, and the closer it got for me to leave, the happier she got. I thought that it was because we had such a great time for three weeks.

It's Sunday night, and my bus was leaving at six thirty p.m. My brother took me to the bus station because Mae's mother was sick, and she wanted to stay with her. However, the ticket was supposed to be for 6:30 a.m., but the clerk had put 1830 p.m. They had the wrong time; my bus left that morning. We had been told before we left basic training that if that happened to call our new assignment, which I did. They told me that I would be leaving the next day at 12:45 p.m. I was happy I could surprise Mae and stay another night, so my brother took me to my sister's house, and I tried to call Mae but got no answer. Knowing that she said her mother was sick, I went to her mother's house to make sure everything was okay, but on my way to her house, I saw her mother who was not sick. So now I was thinking something might be wrong with Mae and continued to her the house. When I was approaching the house, I could see her standing on the steps, leaning over. Thinking she was sick, I rushed to her. She didn't see me coming so I could get close enough to see that she was with a man. I can't honestly say what they were doing, but I can say that if you just left your future husband, you shouldn't be in that position.

I wanted to find out what was going on, and she said that her mother had asked her to keep him company while she was with someone else. This really devastated me. I just stood there for a few seconds and told her I wanted to talk to her. This guy was from the local Air Force base. She had been going with him the whole time I was gone. She said that he was just a friend to her and the nothing happened. I knew she lied. I could tell by the way her clothes were that something happened. The more she lied, the worse my temper got. I couldn't believe that she would do this to me after all the good things that I thought we had. It turned out that it was not true. I even found out later that she had been with my brother too.

I lost it that night. I felt so betrayed I couldn't see straight. She said something that hurt my feeling, and I slapped her hard. The airman took off at that point without even offing to defend her, but from that point, I didn't care and slapped her again, and she wanted to hug me and said that she only did it because her mother had asked her to be with him. Everything she said or every gesture of compassion she offered only made me worse. I just kept hitting her and hitting her. She had a bloody nose and swollen lip. I could see her eye was swelling too. I took her in the house and left and didn't see her for three months. When I did, we talked, but the feeling was gone. Though she bought the first bit of violence out of me, she was the first woman that I was in love with. I tried to give her my undivided attention, but she was not serious about me at all. So we moved on.

I never dreamed that day would turn out to be one of the worse days of my life. I could not get over the fact that I hit her because I thought she was having sex with someone else when I just left. My bus had not left the terminal yet, and there she was with him. I never gave her the benefit of doubt. I know what I saw, and it was something that I would never forget. As a young man, I always thought that if my woman was having sex with another man, I could never trust her again. To me there was no need to talk about it. If you want him, feel free, but I don't want you anymore. Mae was the first woman who I had strong feeling for; the others were just about sex. They were women who didn't want to be seen with me, so there was no pretense of love.

The fact that I had been having sex with someone else's wife and/or girlfriend always bothered me. I knew what I was doing was wrong, but it didn't matter. I was just being guided by their lust. I never considered the husband or the boyfriend's feelings. These men were working, trying to take care of their family; and as soon as they went out one door, I was coming in another. I even remember climbing through the window when the older husband left for work but came back about ten minutes later. Maybe this is why, I told myself. If it happened to me, I would never touch her again.

That became the longest night of my life because I was looking for her mother to call the police and have me arrested for assaulting her daughter. I went to my sister's house and waited. I sat there, just staring at the walls, crying, because I knew that I would be either in jail or leaving town in a few hours. I knew that I would never be with her anymore, not able to hold her the way she liked me to rub her shoulders and neck, gently stroking her to the point that it was more ticklish than massaging. Walking my fingers around her upper body would make her laugh hysterically. I missed her already, and I couldn't tell her I was sorry now, and there wouldn't be another chance for months because I was leaving in a couple of hours.

I needed to tell somebody what I did, not my sister because she would have gone crazy. She might have called the police herself. I didn't want her to know until after I left. About four o'clock in the morning I called my friend, Alice, Mae's cousin. I knew that I could talk to her, and she wouldn't be too judgmental about it. She would be honest and tell me what I should do. When I called, her she said to meet her on her porch. She lived across the street from my sister. She came out to the porch. She was in her nightgown. It was four in the morning, but it was a warm night.

I told her that I had beat up Mae and thought that her mother was going to call the police. She said, "What happened?" and I told her that I had caught her with another man. Alice didn't seem surprised, and she said that Mae had be going with him for several months and that her mother made her be with him. It didn't make me feel any better, and I was starting to get mad all over again. Alice said, "I know she has been with him, and it's her mother that makes her do it, but I can tell you for sure that Mae loves you more than anything. Don't leave her wondering about how you feel. Let her know that you are sorry. Even if you don't want her anymore, tell her how she hurt you and tell her that you are leaving and will write her." I didn't take that advice and went to the bus station, got on my bus, and headed to my next assignment.

I didn't see Mae again for over twenty years and didn't talk to her for about fifty years. That was at my sister's homegoing service. My brother told me that she wanted to talk to me and was waiting upstairs. I went upstairs, and there she was, standing there, leaning on the rail. The first think I thought about was that the last time I was this close to her; she was leaning over a rail.

I said, "Hello, how are you doing?"

"I'm doing good," she said and asked me the same question.

I said that it had been a long time since I saw her. Fifty years, she said.

She said, "I've seen you when you were here a few times, but you didn't see me."

I asked how that happened. She said that Alice would tell her when I was in town, and she would come to her house and see me across the street.

I said, "You mean that you saw me and wouldn't speak to me?"

Her answer was, "I didn't think you wanted to see me because you left, and I never heard from you again."

Even at the age of seventy, she was still very beautiful, slender and shapely body, long legs and dressed very nice. She still is very young-looking with an air of sophistication. I was happy to see her. I mean, after fifty years, you expect some wear and tear, but she looked great. As we talked for a few minutes, the thing that was missing was the warm smile, the glow that she projected, a godly shining. She seemed to bear a lot of problems throughout the years, and it was obvious that she wanted to talk about it. I thought that it was going to be about what happened between us, but it was much more than that.

We stood and talked in the church for a couple of hours. She asked me why had I stopped writing her when I was in basic training.

I said, "I didn't stop writing you. You stopped writing me. I wrote you when I went to Germany but never heard from you."

She said, "When I found out about you and Alice, there was no reason to write."

I said, "What are you about?"

She said, "Alice told me that you and she were going to get married, and she showed me letters that you wrote her."

I told her I never have had anything other than a friendly relationship with Alice, and I always wrote her letters, but never about marrying her.

"She was teasing you. Did you read any of the letters?"

She said, "No, she wouldn't let me read them."

Mae and I talked about four hours that night, and she told me that she would always love me because I was her first boyfriend and showed her and taught her about life. She never mentioned the problem we had, and I never reminded her of it. I didn't know if she didn't remember it or just chose not to talk about it. She did tell me how rough she had it with her first husband and the trouble that they had. She told me about her daughters and granddaughter and medical problems that she had, how hard she had to work and the little thanks she got for helping other people. She talked most of the time, and I listened. It was very clear that she doesn't have friends, close enough to share these personal stories with.

I told her about my wife and that we were about to celebrate forty-nine years of marriage. She got a little quiet and seemed to not want to hear it. Because it appeared to bother her, I moved on to another subject. It was really nice talking to her. When I left her, I felt a lot better about myself because she either forgot what had happened or chose not to bring it up. I know that her life appeared to be much more difficult than mine, and I felt for her. She is a religious person, and I know that will always give her peace. I pray that she can find solace with her family and live the remainder of her life in comfort.

CHAPTER FIVE

Anger Revealed!

WHEN I GOT to Fort Sill, Oklahoma, I was still reeling from what had happened just a few days before when I caught her with that airman. What I had done started to hit me. I just beat up a woman, and now I'm in another state, and no one knew where I was because I only told them that I was going to Oklahoma. I knew that if they wanted me, they could come and get me. The fear that this could happen bought all kinds of things to my mind. The police could show up at any time and charge me with a crime. What would I do, how would I react if they came, or would I try to run?

As I settled into life at Fort Sill, my every thought kept going back to Mae and what I had done to her. I kept thinking, *Will I ever see her again, or will she have me arrested for beating her up?* I was wondering if she was hurt really bad, if there was any permanent damage to her face. If I did see her, what could I say to change things, could I even face her? Things just keep popping in my mind of possibilities, but there were no clear answers. Could I forgive myself for what I did to her?

I thought about the plans we made and how I was determined to make them come true. I had saved $60 a month from my $78 paycheck. I wanted to be ready when I finished advanced training to get married and take her with me wherever I was stationed. I was checking all the things I needed to know so that I wouldn't have to wait too long to set the plan in motion. But none of this mattered anymore because as much as I loved her, I didn't think that I could forget what I saw. The reason didn't matter. I didn't think that I could live with it hanging over us.

It's at this point that my drinking got heavier, and I no longer just drank beer. I started to drink hard liquor and a lot of it. I would drink from the time I got off work until lights out. The booze didn't help; it just kept my problems fresh in my head. For sixteen weeks I wanted to talk to Mae, but I was too afraid to make the call. She couldn't call me even if she wanted to. We didn't have access to telephones in those days.

During the same sixteen-week period, I became more and more angry at myself for trusting her the way I did. The more I drank, the more I blamed her for ending my dream of marrying her. My mind was playing tricks on me. One minute I was accepting responsibility for what happened because I should not have hit her. The next minute I was blaming her because she betrayed my trust and thinking that I never wanted to see her again.

Now I had the drinking to blame for not owning up to my responsibility for what I did. I rationalized but pointed at her what she did and that I did nothing wrong. Of course, I did everything wrong. I was blinded by my love for her, so when I saw her, I didn't think anything or anyone could have stopped me from hitting her. I didn't consider that I should have just turned around and walked away from her because I loved her. On the other hand, I didn't consider that if I hadn't approached them that night, it would have been my secret. I was torn between guilt and justification. It didn't make any sense because one can't replace the other. I was guilty of committing a crime because I beat her, and I knew that was an assault. There was no justification because I knew it was wrong but did it anyway.

I was blinded by my love for her. I was drowning in my sorrow and the knowledge that I would never be married to her, nor would I have a family with her. Mae was the love of my life, but I must realize that what we had was gone forever, never to return. My heart was broken, and my spirit was as low as it could be. I prayed for forgiveness and still couldn't accept that God forgives all our sins, and he gives us power over all our actions.

I was ashamed of what I did and wanted to let her know, but how do you say, "I know I beat you up, but I didn't mean it"? When I think about how sorry I was, there was another thought in my mind, telling me that she deserved it because she cheated, not me. Then anger seemed to take over my consciousness, and then I didn't know which way to think. I felt so mad I wanted to get even. I was glad that I was hundreds of miles away. The anger replaced reality, and my blood pressure rose.

I never knew that I had this much anger inside me. It was like a pent-up rage that had been released. I couldn't think of anything to have caused me to feel this way before. God had blessed me by placing me miles away because I didn't know if I could control myself if I was close to her. No matter what I did or tried to do, I could not get my mind off her. The more I thought about it, the more I felt used and humiliated, and I got madder and madder. I couldn't sleep, I couldn't eat, I couldn't close my eyes without thinking about what she did to me.

I was at Fort Stills to train in missiles. I forget what they were called. I just know that you could push a button and launch missiles all over the world. I wanted to concentrate on my work, but it was hard. My mind was consumed by the thought of Mae cheating on me. Why did she do that to me? Everybody knew that she had another man. Why didn't they tell me? Until this day, Alice is the only person to tell that she knew Mae was involved with someone else. I thought that Alice might be making it up too, but I wanted to believe her more than I wanted to believe Mae.

The days became longer and longer, and I couldn't wait to get off so that I could hit the bars. I was drinking more and more, but I could do my job every day, and there were no problems at work. I knew, though, that I had to get control of myself, so I tried working later, which left me less time to go to the bar. As my drinking increased, so did my anger and rage. I began to get into fights for virtually no reason. And by the grace of God, no one wanted to see me get in trouble because they would say they didn't see anything, so I wasn't disciplined for any fights that I started.

I continued to have a hard time at Fort Sill, but my demons only got worse. I just could not shake what I did. One day I rationalized it, and I'm okay. The next day my guilt was overwhelming. I cry a lot when I'm alone, but never in front of anyone. When I was a child, I found it hard to cry when others were around. It became increasingly difficult to hide my mental state. My sergeant major asked me how I was doing one day, and I said, "Fine, Sergeant Major." His name was White. He said, "Come over here." When I got a few steps closer, he said, "Don't lie to me. How are you doing?" Before I could say a word, he said, "I want to see a smile on that face whenever I see you."

That made me remember that I always had a big smile. Most people would ask me, "What are you smiling about?" It made me feel a bit better about myself. A couple of days later, Sergeant White told me that I was on a special detail on the weekend, so I had to pack enough clothes for five days. He didn't say what the detail was. We met at 4:00 a.m., and he told me that we were going to Texas for a few days, and I was his personal bodyguard. He took me everywhere that weekend, and I didn't pay for anything. He reminded me of how my father would just ride around in the car, talking about anything but troublesome things.

Not one time during that weekend did he say anything about smiling or what was happening on post. He talked about all kinds of fun things like golfing and sports. He took me to a baseball game at the new Astrodome. That weekend I do not remember thinking about my problems. He never asked, and we never talked about it. I couldn't figure out why he took me off base that weekend because I never did any work at all; in fact, it was people waiting on me. We returned to the post on that Tuesday, and he said to me, "I don't want to see you without that smile anymore." I said, "Thanks for the trip," and he said, "You needed it."

The rest of my stay at Fort Sill was much better because I was conscious of smiling when I was in public places, and I surely didn't want Sergeant White to see me not smiling. I still had my demons, and they were active; but because I was thinking about smiling all the time, I could control them more. It was time for me to move on, but I really liked the sergeant major and told him that several times before I left.

CHAPTER SIX

Violent Thoughts

AFTER MY ADVANCED training in Oklahoma, my next assignment was in Babenhausen, Germany. This was the first time that I left the country, but that was fine. The Vietnam War was in full force, and we were taking a lot of causalities, and nobody wanted to go there. I had no idea of what it was like, and I didn't know anyone there, but I don't have a choice of where I went, as I remember they asked us to write down two or three places you would want to go. I think that no one put Germany down as their first choice. I flew to Germany, and some of the troops went by boat. Nevertheless, here I was in a strange land and had no idea what people were talking about.

I hadn't talked to anybody for hours since we landed in Frankfort, Germany. While I was waiting for the train to carry us to our town, I wondered what would I do if I got lost. This German woman was sitting next to me and said hello, and I was shocked. She was married to a soldier and was going to the same post as I was. We talked, and after the trip was over, she said, "I hope that I see you again." I told her that I'm sure she would. I saw her three days later at the gym. We became friends, nothing else, just friends. She did introduce me to a couple of her friends though.

My first day on post I went to play basketball in the gym and met an old friend from Philadelphia, who ran the gym, and it so happens that they needed someone to work there because one of them was rotating out. It was my lucky day because I got the job, and for the next two and a half years, that was my military assignment. All I had to do was make sure there were always some activities for the youth, officer's wives, NCOs and their wives, and work with the German nationals. To top it off, I had my own room and did not have to wear a uniform. It was like royalty.

I was there about eighteen months and was drinking really heavily, and my demons were as active as ever before. I was twenty-one or twenty-two. I would still get letters from Alice and an occasional letter from my brothers and sisters, but I still missed Mae but made no attempt to reach her. We would go to the enlisted men's club most of the time, but we spent some time out with the civilians too. I got to know some of the older people, and they really made me feel like I was at home. Many of them would invite me to dinners and parties. The thing that scared me was whether I should try to date any of their daughters, but the answer to that came in a short manner when one of the biggest businessmen I dealt with had a seventeen-year-old daughter who asked me to go dancing with her. I hesitated, and he said, "She likes you. It is okay. Go have fun."

We went out, and she told me that she could do anything except drink or use drugs, that she was promised by her parents that there were no limits to her partying if she stayed away from those two things. I was the only person of color in the party, but no one seemed to care. Only a few of them spoke English, but none of them said or did anything to make me feel uncomfortable. Maybe I was the only one with different thoughts on his mind. I hung out with Bridgette for a while and enjoyed her company, but we drifted apart and would only get together once or twice a month. I dated a couple of German women for about a year and had fun with them, but because it seemed like they only wanted to party and have sex, it didn't matter to them if you loved them; not all the women are this way. I had been there about a year, working in the gym, giving exercise classes to the wives and Germany nationals.

Then Charlene came on the scene. Man, was she beautiful. Because I worked in the gym, I could go to all the clubs, but occasionally some NCO or officer would kick me out. But one Sunday night this woman was signing a Ray Charles song (*I Can't Stop Loving You*), and I jumped up and said, "I can't either." She took a break and came to our table. Another friend named Ron was with me and said that she wanted him, so they talked, and she went back to the stage and sang a few more songs. We always closed the clubs because we didn't have bed check (curfew), so when the club started closing, we walked slowly out the door, trying to let her catch up. She did, and I said I might go to an after-hour spot. She said, "I'm going where you go," and she asked Ron if he wanted to meet her friend. That was how my relationship with her started, and it was great too. We would sit and talk for hours, and it would be about the ups and downs of life.

As we grew closer, Charlene had said that she had come from some city in Germany where her father was, so I had assumed that she was in Germany with her father. We would meet and talk and make out in my room after the gym closed. Then one day there was a basketball tournament, and she came, so I was thinking she was there to see me. I went over to see her and said, "Nice to see you." She said, "Hi, this is my husband." My mouth flew open, and I didn't know what to do. She said he didn't care about her, and she just wanted to come back to the States. I said that I thought she was here with her father. She said, "I visited my father who was in Germany at the time in the Air Force." I found out that her husband really didn't care too much about her, and I was leaving in four months (being discharged). She asked if she could come with me. I said yes.

I came home and then sent her money to come home. We lived in Delaware with my brother for a few months before I got a place of our own. It was about three months from the time I got home before Charlene came. I picked her and her son up at the airport, and we settled in Delaware for a while. I had gone back to work at General Foods and was making good money but had not gotten our own place yet because we were not sure where we wanted to live.

She was about six months pregnant with our son, and she seemed to be very happy about it. Even though it went against everything I believed, I still was overjoyed. I was going to be a father. That's where our problems really started. I really was happy, but it was hard for me to get over the fact that Charlene had known how I felt about having children out of wedlock and promised that she would use her birth control pills until we were married. Although I only talked to her about it one time, I think that she surmised that I could not get over it. I don't know what I did or if I acted differently, but she would refer to it as her baby. In those days, we didn't have the option of getting the baby's sex, so we didn't know if it were a boy or girl. I just knew I wanted it no matter what the sex was. I couldn't help feeling betrayed when she told me the news, but it was more my fault than hers.

But she knew how I felt about the way I wanted my family to start because I told her about the two things that I always wanted to be in order with my live. I guess because it was something that became sacred to me. The first thing was that I wanted to be married before I had children because that is something that I grew up with. All the people around me were having babies with no husbands and guys not even caring about what the children might have to endure from their peers. I would hear bullies call them bastards and other horrible names.

The second thing, it was very important to me (at the time) that my first son be named after me. I guess because I thought that he would carry on my legacy, so he would name his son Ron the III. I always liked the fact that sons were named Junior and so on.

Since we were sexually active, I should have been more careful, but I depended on her to take her birth control pills to avoid getting pregnant. After all, we talked about it. I did not take any precautions myself I just laid it all at her feet.

When he was born, I was working as a salesman and not at home when she went into labor. It was early evening, and I had to meet with a client in San Francisco that afternoon. When I got home, we rushed to the hospital, and there he was. I was full of joy and excitement. That was the best night of my life so far. I had a smile that never left my face. He was a good baby too. You could feed him and change his diaper, and he would sleep until feeding time came again. I didn't want to call him junior, so I was trying to come up with something that would distinguish us from one another. I thought about calling him O. In those days, I had a lot of options.

A few weeks went by, and the birth certificate came; and when I read it, I told her they put the wrong name on it. Her reply was, "Oh, they did?" and nothing else. I wanted to get it right, so I told her mother (because she worked at the hospital) that I wanted the change it. She said, "I told Charlene that I wanted him to be named after my father, Edward." We never got it changed, and it was a sore spot for me; it still is, but it doesn't matter.

Our problems started to escalate from there, though. I started being annoyed when I came home, and the house was dirty, the baby needed changing, a lot of things that I would take care of, but we had a lot of arguments. After a while, her mother didn't trust me anymore (she said that I was the devil because my eyes were always red). She would be watching me, and I didn't know why. One day she came to our apartment (she just lived a few hundred yards away), and we were arguing about the baby having diaper rash. His diaper was so wet you could wring the water out of it. Her mother (who has passed on now, God bless her soul) said, "Did he hit you again?" and she said yes. She told me that if I ever hit her daughter again, I would regret it. I replied that she was lying. I had never hit before. I swear on a stack of Bibles that I had never laid a hand on her and couldn't understand why she would say that. I could never convince her mother of that. But that's when I decided to get further away from there so we could have more privacy. I thought there was too much interference from her mother, but now I knew why.

I could see that things were deteriorating, so I started to withdraw from her family and do more things alone. I didn't feel comfortable anymore, and I still hadn't made any friends of my own. I started drinking a lot in the following months. It seemed that there was nothing else to do but go to work and come home and have a drink. I never liked to argue, so that was one thing I didn't really do much of; instead I would keep everything to myself. I had no buddies to talk to. I would call my brother every now and then. He could sense that I was depressed because he once said to me, "You should always call one of your brothers or sister when you don't have any one to listen to you. You know that you will get the truth from us." He, too, has passed on. He said, "God will listen to you. Call on him, talk to him, and you will get the answer to your problem." My brother was a preacher, so that's what you expect to hear from him.

I was not as angry about him not having my full name as I was about how Charlene had just ignored my wishes, and it was all about pleasing her mother rather than my feelings. This was the woman that I wanted to spend the rest of my life with, but I could see that if we were close to her mother, it would get worse. I told Charlene that I could get a transfer with the phone company to Southern California and wanted to take the opportunity. She thought that was a good idea and seemed happy about the move, but we started talking about a business of our own. I knew a lot about the trucking industry and had told her before that someday I might buy a truck and trailer. She thought it was a good idea, but she, too, saw that the interference from her mother would always be present and thought it would be better if we left too. We planned for several months on how to start the business, and I was talking to a person in Delaware who had a trucking business who was encouraging me to come back there and help him; we would be partners.

It was her idea that we move back to Delaware. I would start the trucking company and build our house and live there. Since Reno was close, we're going to spend our first night on the road there. We were going to get married then tell everybody because we didn't want to give anyone the chance to talk us out of it. So as the days got closer, we kept our secret and planned or move back east. We set up the movers, and I was trying hard to get a transfer to the phone company in Dover Delaware. However, I couldn't transfer, but one of the top executives here was from Delaware, and he arranged for me to be hired there. Not one time leading up to our departure date did either of us express any regrets about the move. I went to work for the last time. I said goodbye to all my coworkers and spent the whole day wondering if the movers were there and if everything was going okay. It was a nerve-racking experience.

When I got home around three o'clock, the house was empty. Everything went well. Charlene wasn't home, and I figured that she was probably out, getting some last-minute shopping done. I lay down on the floor and fell asleep for a couple hours. When I woke up, she still wasn't there. It was about five thirty, so I called her mother to see if she was at her house. The first thing she said to me was, "She's not here, and don't call anymore. I'm not getting in this mess." I said, "What mess?" She told me that I couldn't be beating on her and expect her to go with me. (Still at that time I had never hit her, even playing.)

Now I was going crazy because I didn't know what is happening. All I knew was that I expected the furniture to be gone, and I always let her handle all the money; that's why I had only four dollars in my pocket. I had no food or anything. I had quit my job, and now I had nothing. A couple days went by, and her mother told me that she was all right but didn't want to see me, but I had a chance to tell her that I never hit her daughter. She listened but didn't believe me. She didn't tell me where Charlene was, but even though she still didn't like me much, I think she could tell I was right. After all, I asked her if she ever saw any marks on her. She said, "No, not really."

After about six weeks, I got a note from Charlene, asking me to call her (she sent it to our old address, and it was forwarded to me), so I got happy because maybe I would find out what went wrong, or maybe we would get back together. I was living in a rooming house then, so she wanted to come by and see if things were okay. I agreed to that. When she came by, we talked about twenty minutes and were in bed, making love. She said that she loved me but wanted to take some time to get settled in her new place. She came to my place a couple of times a week, but one day her mother saw me talking to her and told me to leave her alone. She said, "She doesn't want you anymore, so you need to stop bothering her. How did you find out where she lived anyway?" I said that she told me when she came to my place that I could come and see my son. Well, she didn't know that we were seeing each other and asked her daughter why she was coming to my place. She said that the sex was good, and she wanted it. That's when I think her mother knew that I had not been beating her.

My birthday was coming up, and Charlene invited me over for dinner. She said that she would cook a good meal for me because I was so skinny. She wanted to do it on Saturday because my birthday was on Monday. I was so glad that I was going to see my son and her son too. She had an eight-year-old son from another marriage. He and I used to have a lot of fun together. The Friday before the big day, she came over, and we spent about five hours together because she said that she would be busy all day Saturday. It was so satisfying that we were getting back together.

Well, it was Saturday, and I couldn't wait to get there. Seemed like there were forty hours in that day, but it was time to go and see the boys. But it didn't go that way when I got there. What a surprise, she had another man and his friend there, and she introduced him as her boyfriend and asked me why I was there. I said, "You invited me for my birthday so that I could see Ronnie and Melvin [who were approaching me by then]." I reached down to pick him (Ronnie) up, and the boyfriend told me not to touch him. We got into a big argument, just verbal, but loud. About five minutes later, here comes the police, and she told them that I had come to her house and started a fight with her boyfriend. They took me off the jail and charged me with disturbing the peace. I was in jail for about four hours, growing madder and madder by the minute. My boss from the telephone company where I had just quit bailed me out. But I had left my car keys in her house and had to go back.

All hell broke out. We started fighting, and she jumped on my back to protect her boyfriend. I grabbed the knife that he had in his hand and lunged at him. I just started swinging at them. He ran, and I just wanted to kill her. Why did she treat me like this? All I did was to try and make a good life for us, and she kept lying about me at every turn. She was willing to send me to jail to be with someone she had known for three days. I cut her hands and wrist, but I probably would have killed her if it hadn't been for the two boys yelling,

"Daddy," and her son asking me to stop. That was the only thing that saved her life and mine that night. I was so angry. Why is it that the two women I felt the closest with turned on me when I had done nothing to deserve it? I always did the best I could for them. I gave them everything that I thought they wanted but still was unable for them to concentrate on me as I had done for them.

I had nowhere to go. The only people I really knew here was her family or friends. I finally decided to go to our old apartment complex because my neighbor, whom I had played chess with, was there. I think his name was Jim. He noticed right away that there was something wrong and asked, "Bibi, what's going on with you?" I told him that I thought I might have killed Charlene and told him what had happened. He asked me if I wanted him to contact anyone, and I said no, but thanks. Jim said that I could stay there that night and fixed a bed for me. I knew he was scared but never said anything about what I should do. He just listened until I finished telling him about the night.

Monday afternoon I was arraigned and formally charged with AWDW (assault with a deadly weapon), and bail was set at fifteen thousand dollars, which I didn't have. Still thinking that she was going to die, I just knew that I would get a life sentence. On the way back to the jail, my emotions got the best of me. I started crying and couldn't stop. I mean I had tears running down my face, and I couldn't wipe them away because my hand was shackled around my waist and feet. One of the guards told me that if the inmates saw me crying that they would try to take advantage of me. He said, "Try to get a hold of yourself." He was right. No sooner than I got put in a cell, this one guy came and said, "Give me your cigarettes." I gave him one, but he wanted them all. At that time, another inmate asked me what I was in there for. I said that I had murdered my girlfriend in a fight a couple of days before. That got me some space from the bully, and they kept telling me that I might get life. Man, I could not stop crying every time I thought about it; the tears just started flowing.

When I went back to court, I was assigned an attorney because I couldn't afford one; but he told me that he was not going to be my attorney, that he would appoint one, but he said to me, "You're looking at some serious charges." Still I didn't know that she was alive and that most of the wounds were to her hands and arms (this is not meant to minimize the injuries at all). About two weeks later, my attorney finally came to see me, and the first thing he said was that we would plead guilty to a lesser charge and maybe get me probation. I told him that I wanted to know who had my son, and he said that he would have his secretary call and see if his mother would allow me to have that information. I said that it was his mother that I killed. He looked surprised at first, then he said, "You're not charged with killing anybody. Why do you think you were here for murder?" I said when I told one of the trustees that I was charged with AWDW, he told me that it was murder and that I was facing a life sentence. He laughed really hard and then said that inmates play jokes to young people who are new to the system.

For the next three months, I set there in jail, waiting for the trial to start. My brother sent me money to get an attorney because he didn't want me to use the public defender; however, I ended up giving that fifteen hundred dollars to an inmate who was getting out, and he was going to take it to the attorney for me. I never saw that money or attorney and never saw the inmate again. I couldn't even remember his name.

So my trial date came, and when I went to court my, public defender didn't even know my name, and I was so scared that he would not do a good job (after all, I had never even had a need for an attorney before, so I didn't know what they would do). But I had made up my mind that I was not going to lie about what happened. The one thing that I had not lost was my sense of responsibility. I knew what I had done was wrong, and I needed to pay my debt to society. I just didn't understand how our judicial system worked.

That first day they called several witnesses who all testified against me. Most of them told the truth as they knew it, but a couple of them who were not there made up stories based on what they were told. It lasted about three hours, and I didn't have anyone to speak on my behalf, so there was not much that the public defender could do. So I now thought that I would surely spend a lot of time in prison.

During the lunch break, my attorney told me that we didn't have anything but my word against all the prosecution witnesses. I told him that I just wanted to tell my side of the story, and he said, "Did you do it?" I told him the truth, yes, I did it, but it didn't happen the way they were saying it did. I said that they jumped on me, and I lost it; and when I realized it, I had the knife and was hacking away at them. Her son and the baby were crying and tugging at my legs. When I saw them, I just ran away.

My attorney said to me, "If you want to take responsibility, you have the option of pleading guilty. The judge will let you tell your side, and because you don't have any prior arrest, he will give you time served and put you on probation, and if you don't have any more arrest during the probationary period, everything will be expunged from your record, and it will be as if you never had a conviction." He told me to ask my family to write a letter to the judge and tell him about my character so that he would know something about my life. He said that he would do what he could to get me released from jail as soon as he could. I decided to take his advice. After all, I was guilty, but I didn't want to be portrayed as a monster. But it would take another three weeks before I went back to court for sentencing.

This following information is very important because it was the first positive thing to happen in months. Over the years, I began to think that because of this sentencing date in court, I could keep some perspective in my life and not stray off into the world of hatred and crime. I could live up to my responsibilities, and though I had nothing, I held the feeling that I could come back.

I was facing a judge that was said to always give the maximum sentence allowed by law so I wasn't too optimistic about what would happen, but I had some hope now. Court proceedings are unpredictable, and the day just dragged on and on. I got a message that I would be due in court at two o'clock in the afternoon. I really started to tear up and felt overwhelmed again, not knowing what was going to happen to me. Would I get a long prison term, or would I be released in short order?

When the judge came into the courtroom, I broke into a heavy sweat and started shaking and was visibly nervous. The judge was an older gentleman with graying hair, thick glasses, but he looked kind of pleasant to me. The judge called my name, and my turn had finally arrived. "Mr. Brokenbrough, you are charged with violating section [I don't remember the number] AWDW of the California penal code. How do you plead?"

My reply was, "Guilty, Your Honor."

He said, "Has anyone told you or promised you anything to plead guilty?"

I said, "No, sir, I committed the crime, but I just wanted you to know that I was defending myself. I didn't know that it was her on my back."

The judge said to me, "Sir, you are a good man. I have a lot of letters from people who support you, and I think they are right. I have a letter from two very important people at the phone company who have known you for just over a year, asking that I not send you to prison. Did you ask them to write me?"

I said, "No, sir, I only asked my sisters and brothers and no one else."

"Well," he said, "every letter says what a kind and gentle person you are, and I have only talked to you for a few minutes, and I feel that you don't deserve to be sent to prison. I'm going to sentence you to four months in the county jail and place you on probation for three years. How do you feel about that?"

I was extremely happy to know that I was not going to prison for some years.

I said, "That's fine, sir, thank you."

The judge continued reading the sentencing, saying, "You have been in the county jail for a little over three months, so with the time served, you will have about twenty days left to do. I don't want to see or hear from you again [which I don't think I will]. If you violate the terms, you must serve out the remaining time in jail. If you complete the terms after three years, the crime will be reduced to misdemeanor and expunged from your record. It will be as if you had not committed any crimes. Do you have anything to say?"

I said that I was sorry for what I did and didn't mean to hurt anyone, and I would not bother her or her family anymore.

With that done, and I no longer had to worry about how long I would be in prison, I felt like I could start over and put my life back together. I thought that I would not have another chance, so I was not going to mess anymore.

As for Charlene and her family, I didn't hear from them for a while, but one day I saw her mother at the store; and to my surprise, she spoke to me. I was not sure what to do or what to say to her because of what I had done. I never thought that she would be that friendly to me because the last time I saw her was in court, and she was not happy with me. She never said anything to me about what happened. She asked me when I got out of jail. I said that was released about two weeks ago. She told me, "You need to try and get yourself together so that you can be in your son's life. He needs his father, and I know you love him." I told her that I didn't want to cause any problems with Charlene, and Margret said it's not about her. She told me, "When you're ready to see him, call me, and I will bring him to you." I said that I really missed him and would love to see him, and she gave me her phone number and told me, "I don't want him to see you like this." This was a point in my life that I thought would never come about. I never expected that she would approach me under any circumstances, but she did, and I thought it was one of the blessings that I had asked of God. I thanked her and committed to being in his life. I knew that I could count on her to keep her word.

After a while, I had opportunity to tell Margret that I was sorry and thank her for talking to me. I offered her an apology and told her that I did not mean for that to happen. She looked at me and said, "I didn't know that Charlene was lying to me about you beating her. I thought she was afraid of you, but she wasn't." After that, we had a normal relationship. Margret and I were friendly after that because she loved her family, and she wanted Ron to be part of my life too.

This just took me back to Mae and why I was so mad at her. She was having an affair, and it destroyed me. I thought that it was the worst thing that you could do to someone, but I wasn't thinking about what happened to the other men when I was with their wives. Even though I was still upset about what Mae had done two years before, I was still doing it to someone else. While I was still angry at Mae, I had settled down a bit and had not gotten angry at any of the women that I'd dated here. I tried to get myself together, but the drinking was taking over. Every minute I had to myself was spent drinking and getting drunk. I got drunk every night, went to bed, and was up bright and early in the morning. Self-pity had also become a factor in my daily routine; everybody was against me. Nobody cared about what I thought. They always took the side of the other person. I had no one to talk to because I didn't have any friends. They were all her friends. Those were the times when I was most lonely; that's when I would lock myself in my room and cry for hours. I needed someone to tell me what to do. I had no one, and when somebody asked me, "How are you doing, do you need anything?" I would say, "I'm fine. No, I don't need anything."

I was crying and suffering through this mental anguish and wouldn't allow anybody to help me. Then I was complaining because I didn't have anyone to talk to. My foolish pride was the major factor in me being alone, telling people that I didn't need any help while wondering why no one would help me. My brothers and sisters would help if they knew I needed them. My father would send me money from time to time, but I lied to him too. I was too ashamed to let them know that I was basically homeless. They would have said, "Come home," and I could stay with them and their family. But they didn't know how bad I was. They still knew me as that well-mannered, clean-cut, quiet brother who they had not seen for almost three years. Instead of telling them about myself, I preferred searching for soda bottles and turn them in for the deposit to buy a can of tuna or a couple slices of bologna and crackers.

I rationalized my condition by telling myself, I'm not a drug addict, so I'm not as bad as they are. All I do is drink and get drunk, but tomorrow I will be okay. But tomorrow would produce the same results. I'd get up, drink a beer, and go job-hunting. Then I would find some soda bottles to get something to eat and buy a couple beers or some whiskey then go home and sulk at my life. At some point, I thought things through and realized that I was a drug addict. The booze had control over me because when I was searching for soda bottles to sell, the first thought was to find enough bottles so that I could buy some liquor too. I knew I had a problem, but could I work on it in my current position? This was another bit of information that consumed my thinking, but I didn't do anything to change it. I thank God that it stayed on my mind; it was a reminder that I needed to fix this problem too.

CHAPTER SEVEN

The Transition!

WHERE DO I go?

After I had served the remaining twenty days of my sentence, I was released from jail with no place to go and no money in my pocket. I had to sleep in my car for about three days. I was afraid to ask my brothers for more money, so I tried to find a job so that I could get a place to live. I would gather soda bottles (you could get three cents for each bottle) every day so that I could buy some bologna and crackers to eat. It wasn't hard to find them in those days, and there weren't too many people searching for them either. Remember that this was in 1970, and things were a lot cheaper then. You could buy bologna for about ten cents a pound.

I finally used a nickel to call my father (we called him Daddy) to let him know that I was all right (he never wanted me to leave home), and we talked about what I was going to do. I told him that I wanted to stay and find a job, but I didn't have any money yet. Daddy said, "I don't have much, but I will send you what I can." He told me to find a Western Union where he could send the money. The next day I called and gave him the address, and later that day he sent me three hundred dollars. I could see that I was being blessed with things I needed to get on the right track, and I didn't want to blow it. I always knew that my father would do anything he could for all his children, but I could tell too that it really hurt him when he knew that I was homeless.

With the money I got from my father, I could get some of the things that I needed, especially a haircut, which led to more blessings. The barbershop that I went to get a haircut was owned by a lady who owned the house that I lived in before I was locked up. She had a few rooms to rent. She had several houses where she rented rooms to people and had one available, so I rented a room from her. She would talk to me all the time and knew that I didn't have much money, so she told me that I should get on welfare until I could find a job. I told her I didn't want to be on welfare, but she told me if it bothers you, just pay the money back when you get a job. I liked that idea and went to the welfare department and asked them questions about lending me the money, and I would pay it back.

They told me, "Yeah, you can always pay us. We wish more people would think that way." They gave me a welfare check, but I had to check in every week to show them that I was looking for a job. I can't remember how much I received; I think it was around thirty-five or forty dollars on the first and the fifteenth of the month. I received these checks for about three months before I got a job. When I did get a job, the pay was above average, and I had way more than I was spending at that time, and I went to repay the welfare and was told that they would set up a payment schedule for me. I never could get those payments set up to repay what I had been given. Eventually I just quit trying. I asked a person who worked as a social worker for the county about why I couldn't set up the payments. She said, "We give people the assistance because they need it. The only way we make you pay it back is if you received through fraud."

I could not thank my landlady enough for everything that she had done for me. She was the first person sympathetic to my situation. She told me that I was wrong; "But it's done, and you can't undo it, so you need to prove to yourself that the next time you can walk away and let her go." She was a very strong mentally and very forceful doing business transactions. She would ask me every day, "Did you eat today?" I would say yes. "Okay, what did you eat?" she would ask. For several months, she would check on me three or four times a week. Sometimes she would just start me talking about something then would listen mostly while I expressed myself about what I wanted to do and about my son. After a while, she would say, "Now, don't you feel better when you talk about it?"

A few months had passed, and my landlady started telling me that once I can talk to Charlene without thinking that she will take me back, I should explain to her what caused me to commit such an act of violence against her. She said that she would understand and start to feel more comfortable around me. "It doesn't matter what you say caused it. Charlene needs to know that you regret it." Well, I did just that when I saw Charlene thirteen years later. I told her that I just lost it, and I have gotten better control of my temper.

My landlady, Lola, was right, but the surprise came when I was telling her about our conversation. She said, "I knew that she would understand because I understood the person who shot me six times, and if I can do it, so could she and any other woman, or man, for that fact. She loves making people do things that they would not normally do, so if the person ever had any feeling for you, they will be more likely to forget what happened over time." She was shot six times in the chest and stomach and lived to tell about it. But most of all, even though I didn't follow her advice completely, I have come to see over the years that she was spot on. I always knew that it would be a long shot. Even talking to Charlene again made me feel like I had been relieved of a great burden. I am truly sorry about what happened, and now I think she believes that I am too.

It is March 1970, and I am still looking for a job. I still don't have much money, so I take regional transit to downtown and visit several potential employers whom I have preselected for that day. My landlady had a nephew who also lived in one of her rooming houses. One day she asked me to move from the house where I had been staying because she was selling it, but I could move into the house that she had about a block away. I had no choice but to comply with her request because I had no place else to go, and she hadn't given any of the other people the choice of moving in the other house. I literally walked with my bags from one house to the other.

That's where I met Fred (her nephew). He was my age but a big man, standing about six feet four inches tall and weighing no less than 250 pounds. He was a very gentle person, easy to talk to, and I could tell right away that he didn't have a violent thought in his mind. If he did, he did an excellent job hiding it. Fred had a good job and was very obedient. I could always hear him leaving for work every day, just wishing that I had the opportunity to show someone that I had the same kind of work ethics.

Fred and I would soon become very good friends. He is the kind of person that I could trust because he had no hidden agenda. If he told you something, he thought it was the truth. I can't recall Fred ever telling a lie about anything. He had a girlfriend and spent most of his time of with her. She lived in another city, so when he was off, he would be gone. What I liked about him most was that he didn't judge me either even though he knew what I had done. He never said anything derogatory about me; that is his nature.

One day he asked me if I wanted a job. (I think that he had to choose between me and his first cousin which one of us he wanted to tell about the opening.) I said I did, and he told me about an opening at his employer. I went to put in the application and was hired. I know that they took his word about me because the questions they asked were mostly about my character and not work experience. I couldn't thank Fred enough for what he did for me. Little did he know how important that reference was to me. It wasn't just about getting a job, but it had to do everything with shaping my life. The day that I got that job was like a revelation to me. I am not a lost cause. I can recover.

In the boarding house with Fred and me were Larry, Harvey, and Buddy. During this time, I had become a heavy drinker. Harvey and Buddy were heavy drinkers and always had booze on hand. And though they all drank, Harvey was the worst drinker. Buddy was next, and I was the third heaviest drinker. I went to work every day, but I had my drinks every night too. I don't remember Fred ever taking a drink. Occasionally Larry drank very little. They all had their girlfriends, and I didn't have one at that time. So much of the time I was either a tagalong or just stayed at home.

One day Buddy said to me, "I have a cousin in Arkansas. You would like her, and she don't have a boyfriend either."

I said, "I don't like women from Arkansas because they dip snuff and chew tobacco and be spitting all over the place."

He said, "I don't think she does that. All I know is that you would like her."

I said, "Okay, if she ever comes to California, I will meet her."

He said, "Okay, I will ask my sister if you can come to dinner Saturday night."

I said, "Tomorrow is Saturday."

He said, "Yeah, she got here a week ago."

So at this point in my life, I can see things are getting back close to normal.

So Saturday night came, and I went with Buddy to his sister's house for a party, which they had already planned to meet his cousin from Arkansas. Suddenly I started feeling a little nervous for the first time in my life. I was going on a blind date. I didn't really have anything to offer. Just got a job. Still don't have any extra money. What am I going to talk about? I didn't have to worry about my clothes. In those days, all my suits were tailor-made and were a perfect fit, and I had very expensive shoes. I knew that I would look good, but what would I say that would make her give me her attention? When we got there, his sister and cousin were not there; so we started to have a drink, but I thought that I didn't want her to think that I was a drunk and told Buddy that we should wait.

They finally came in about an hour later, and his cousin never made eye contact with me, and now the nerves were really shot. It was as if she had told them that she didn't want to meet me, and they tricked her into coming. I didn't know what to do. She was thin, stood about five feet three or four inches, and couldn't weight more than ninety pounds. Her body was shaped like a model's: large breast, small waistline, and her hips were just the right size for her frame. Dressed in a short skirt and blouse, she was neat, but it was a very modest skirt—not too short—and the blouse not cut too low. When Buddy got around to introducing us, he said, "This is my friend Ronnie," but said, "what is your last name?" I knew he couldn't pronounce it, but he knew it. I said my name, and he said, "This is my cousin Dorothy Nell. She said hello and went right back to the kitchen. For the next two hours, she was in the kitchen with Katherine, her cousin. I was just sitting there, feeling stupid. I didn't know what to say. One of my greatest fears is that a woman would say something embarrassing to me, and I would never be the same again.

By this time, I have had a few drinks, but I wasn't close to being drunk. I went over to the bar that separated the kitchen from the family room and asked her to dance. Her reply was, "No thanks," and my thoughts were beginning to throw me into a state of sorrow. I was thinking, *Why did I agree to this?* I had to do something to get her talking. She has been there now for two hours and only spoke to answer questions, never to strike up a dialogue. I just sat back down and waited, hoping that there would be some event that would get us to talking.

It was getting late, and I was feeling that the whole night was spent doing nothing, but I wanted to talk to her now just to see why she had nothing to say all night. As I got up and walked across the room to where she was sitting, I felt in a devilish moment coming on.

I walked over to her and said, "Well, it's been about two hours now, and you know that you love me so we should go get married."

She started laughing and said, "I don't even know you. How could I be in love with you?"

I said, "Because I told you," and started acting like I was putting a spell on her.

That got her to talking, denying that she had any feels for me. The rest of the night went on just fine.

Dorothy had been married before and had a son, nine-year-old Tony. You could tell right away that she put everything she had into making sure that he had what it wanted. He was her only child, and she was her father's only child, so they both got pretty much what they wanted. But you never got the idea that she blocked everybody out of her life because she a single mother. Tony took an instant liking in me also, and he seemed to be raised well even though you could see that he got mostly what he asked for.

We dated for a while before I met her father—without a doubt one of the best men that I have ever met in my life. They called him JB. He was a quiet man, and from the first minute I saw him to his death some twenty years later, he never changed. JB had been in the construction industry, working as a pipefitter for a major company in Sacramento. His income was always above the average, and he has invested in a home and property and lived in the same area for many years, so he was well known in his community. He never said much, but the thing that we had in common was that we both loved his daughter and were big San Francisco Giants fans, so the most conversation would be about them.

I could tell right away that he liked me too. No one really knew me, and I know that they were cautious of how they dealt with me, but he never wavered in any way about how he felt. As our relationship grew, so did our partying and drinking. It seemed like every weekend we would be drinking and getting drunk. I never tried using any drugs or narcotics because I had a fear of getting hooked on some drug and have my life destroyed like others that I have seen. So as far as I was concerned, I could drink my Hennessey's and my Hamm's beer, and I was cool. I could get drunk on Saturday, sleep Sunday, get up and go to work on Monday, and wait for the next weekend to come.

Little did I know that I was becoming addicted to the drug in the bottle. I would drink beer every night and, on the weekend, hard liquor. This went on week after week, and I was out. Pacing my friends, by far, no one was drinking as much as I did. The more I drank, the less tolerant I became with anything. I couldn't stand it when I thought someone was patronizing me or if you could not understand my point of view. It soon got to the point that I started withdrawing into my little shell, but I would still go out and drink and get drunk with them; but the only thing that was wrong with that is that no one else was getting drunk but me and Dorothy.

This might sound boring to you, but it is necessary to recount the events as close to accurate as possible because I don't want this to be become just something that I wrote. I want to be a teaching moment that there are a lot of men and women experiencing the guilt. There is a lot of pain that still needs relieving, and the only way to do that is to continue spilling my guts in a truthful manner. You see, I was so self-conscious of not getting involved with hard drugs I was consumed by the most common drug of them all—alcohol. This almost destroyed my life, and it could have landed me in prison because my temper had gotten to the point that I was not going to be cast aside until you heard my side of the story. That is why I thank God every day for bringing a man like JB into my life. I was living with his daughter, and he knew that things were not what they should have been, but he never told me that if I touched his daughter that he would kill me or would have someone me beat up. Although I know he would have if I had hurt her bad. What he did do was to ask me to go with him to do something but would just ride around town sometimes for hours, then he would take me back home. JB did not talk a lot. We spent a lot of time a talking about the giants and the fact that when he was upset, going for a drive always gave him time to think.

CHAPTER EIGHT

Dorothy

Dorothy

DOROTHY AND I hit it off good, and we started dating; although we didn't call it dating. We just started doing things and going places together. We would go to parties, sometimes to a club. I didn't like clubs too much because there were too many fights. We spent most of the time going to house parties with or friends on Friday or Saturday night. Or we would take Tony the park. I would gather soda bottles so that we could buy a can of tuna, some chips, and some sodas; or she would make some Kool-Aid, and we would set there eating our tuna sandwiches and potato chips. All I had was my 1963 Ford convertible with holes in the roof, but we did have some transportation, and we could go to the drive-in theater when we had the money. Dot would make some hot dogs because we couldn't afford to buy them at the drive-in. Those were the best hot dogs ever. She would wrap them in the plastic wrap and then the aluminum foil, and they would still be warm two hours later.

Our drinking together was not working, and neither one of us had given a thought to what was happening to us. Although I don't think they meant it in a deceitful way, I became entertainment for our friends. They knew that once I got drunk, they would have a good laugh. One woman told me, "Ron, you sure are funny when you get drunk." That comment never left my mind. The thought ran through my mind that they really didn't care about me; they just liked the way I acted a fool when I got drunk. And the truth is that those words helped me tremendously because the more I thought about them, the more I was concerned about what they thought of me, and the less I wanted to be thought of as funny only when I was drunk. I know that they didn't mean that as an insult, but only after I had thought about it for quite some time.

I moved in with her because she had a house, and I was still living in the rooming house. We didn't have any money, so we couldn't do much, only things that didn't cost us. But we made the best of what we had. We knew a lot of people who had a lot less than we did. I always thanked the Lord for everything that he gave us. Dot was a good housekeeper. It was always clean, and she seemed to enjoy what she had. I would come home from work, and the music was so loud you could hear it a half block away. My first thought would be that Dot's cleaning the house.

Sometimes Tony and I would go fishing while she did what she was doing. She said, "Are we having fish for dinner?" because she knew that we never caught too many fish. Tony would blame me for us not catching anything. He would even tell me, "Pop, why don't you wait for a while before you start fishing?" He would say, "Pop, let me go first because after you fish, they are full and won't bite anymore." Sometimes we did catch a few fish that we could keep, and it was fun teasing each other about their exploits while fishing. She would cook them, and we enjoyed the feast. Tony and I would have our eating contest to see who could eat the most fish and fries, mostly fries. She could cook some chicken too. We would buy chicken wings for ten pounds for a dollar. Dot would cook them, and Tony and I would eat until we couldn't move.

Ronnie was with his mother, so most of the time, it was just Tony and me. When Ronnie was with us, Tony like spending time with him. He was the little brother that he wanted. It made him feel worth something because he could show him how to do things. The two of them really enjoyed each other.

I can even remember what our first fight was about. We were both drunk. We drank all the time. She drank on the weekend, and I drank every day. The way I remember it is that it was another Saturday night, and we had been out somewhere. I thought that she had gotten too close to Larry, one of my friends. She was so drunk she didn't even know where she was, and I was probably worse. But I saw her touching him where she shouldn't. It really made me mad, and I told her about it. She said that she didn't, and that made me worse. I was sitting here, looking at her, and she said that I was lying. I said I was going home, but she didn't want to go; and we had a huge argument about it, and it just wouldn't go away. We went home, and she kept grabbing me by the collar; and eventually I pushed her hard, and she flew into me like a wildcat. I slapped her, and she just kept on going at me. Finally, I hit her again and again until she stopped trying to scratch me in my face. I think she had a black eye the next day, and we didn't talk. She fixed my breakfast, lunch, and dinner, but we never talked.

I really didn't know what I had seen, but that night the alcohol was telling me what to say and how to act. I thought about it for a long time and decided that when I'm sober, I am wrong, but when I'm drunk, I am right. I did a couple things when I was drunk and didn't even know it. It was me trying to rationalize my actions and making excuses for whenever I got into it with her.

A couple weeks had passed when again we were drinking, and something else came up; and boom, here we are, fighting again. I just knew that every time I would say something to her, she would lose control and would always start trying to fight me, and I was too stupid to not fight back. I was much bigger and stronger and knew that she was no match for me, but every time I responded by physically knocking her around. In my mind, I would only be hitting her two or three times, but I really didn't know. I thought that I wasn't really hurting her because she never really showed any real marks or discomfort. I blamed it on the fact that we were both drunk and that the next time I wouldn't let her bait me into hitting her. You see, that's what it became to me—that she was baiting me into these fights, and if she would just keep her hands off me, it wouldn't escalate into physical violence. This was where I started telling myself that it was not my fault; if she didn't hit me, I wouldn't hit her.

We had been together for about six months, and I didn't like the idea of living together, so we decided to get married and went to Reno that weekend and got married. We still didn't have much money, so it was just a small wedding with Fred and Katherine. I even had to borrow ten dollars from him to pay for the preacher. She had already rented a house by her cousin, but there wasn't much furniture. I still had my job, so I applied to a store to buy some living-room furniture, which was about three hundred dollars. When the creditor called my job, the plant manager called me into his office and told me that he got a call and wanted to talk to me about it. I said fine. First, he told me about a guy who had been working there for thirty years and wanted to buy a house, but he told the creditor that he was a part-time employee; he didn't get the house.

Then he told me, "You should wait to buy furniture because you are young and don't really know how to handle your money yet."

I said, "We need some furniture to sit on. We don't have any."

He said, "I'm telling you not to go into debt. You can always get furniture later."

I kind of blew my stack and told him, "I don't need you to tell me how to spend my money. If you had a problem, that's your fault, not mine."

"Young people need somebody to guide them through these things."

I told him that he was not my father, and I didn't need his advice. When I did, I would ask for it. The next week I got laid off. The week before he had laid out all the things that he wanted me to do at the plant for the next six months. They were suddenly no longer that important. I knew he laid me off because I told him that I didn't need him to tell me what to do. I didn't know how to tell Dorothy that I had gotten fired, so I pretended that everything was all right. I thought Fred would tell her cousin (her cousin was Fred's girlfriend), and she would tell Dorothy. It was shocking that he took pride in telling people how to spend their hard-earned money. I would have understood if the credit was for something I didn't need, but we had no furniture. Three weeks later, he hired me back to do the job that I had been doing. He would call me back to work for two or three weeks then lay me off again.

I think that was when things got worse for me at home. After I had lost my job and everything seemed to be spiraling out of my control, I immediately started looking for a job; but in those days, you had to take a test for almost any position, and that took time. I was receiving fifty-three dollars every week in unemployment benefits, which was not nearly enough to take care of the household. I had never been in this position before that I could hardly make ends meet. I took the bus to interviews and spent a lot of time walking the street, looking for something to do. The applications that I did put in were weeks away from being filled, and there was no day work to speak of in those days. But still every day I would get up and go out looking for a job with no success, but I couldn't stop. I have a wife and stepson now, and I have a two-year-old son. I wanted to provide for them. The only way that I knew how to get a job was to walk the street and talk to as many potential employers as I could.

Saturday night, about ten o'clock, just two weeks later, I got a call from another application; this one was from the largest dairy-processing company in the state at the time. They wanted me to start on Monday. All I had to do was pass a physical and go to work. The pay was even better than the city, and the work seemed easier. My start time for this job would be three thirty in the afternoon to eleven at night. I could catch the bus both ways. They gave us uniforms to wear and rubber boots and gloves. All I had to do was go to work and make four dollars and seventy-one cents an hour, which was top-of-the-line pay in 1971. I took this job over the city job.

The city of Sacramento had called me to work, picking up garbage, but I didn't want that job because I didn't think that I could handle those heavy garbage cans. I gave him some excuse about why I couldn't come to work. I think that I told him, "I don't have a car and can't get to work." He said, "Okay, thanks." I didn't have a job, but that wasn't what I applied to the city for; and though he told me that I would be placed in the job when it became available, I did not want it.

On Wednesday, the first week on the new job, I got a call from the city again. He told me who he was and that he had talked to me the week before. I said, "Yes, sir, I remember," and he repeated our conversation then said, "I have found a ride for you. One of my supervisors lives just down the street from you, and I have arranged for him to pick you up and bring you to work every day. You will have the same schedule as he does." I never thought that I would hear from him again, so I put it out of my mind. I didn't know what to say, so I just told him that I wouldn't be able to take that job now because I was going to be leaving the city for a while. He said, "When are you coming back?" I said in about three months. He said, "Okay, I will check with you then." I was sitting there, watching the television one day, and the phone rang, and it was him. He said, "I'm still-ing holding that job for you. Are you ready?" I couldn't believe that he had done that, so I broke down and told him that I didn't think that I could handle those heavy cans. He said, "How do you know?" I told him that I had a friend who outweighed me by eighty pounds doing that job, and he was so tired he couldn't do anything else. I also told him that I had gotten another job. He said, "Good. I tell you what I'm going to do. I will put your name on the inactive list, and if things don't work out for you there, you won't have to restart over here." I said thanks, and he said good luck, but I got a call every time they were hiring and finally got a call, saying it had been two years, and they had to take my name off the inactive list.

Just these two events in my life made me feel that I was meant to be successful and that there was something that people could see in me. It is hard to explain, but throughout my whole life, complete strangers would tell me their innermost secrets. Men and women would walk up to me and strike up a conversation, and before I knew it, they would be crying on my shoulder. I liked that fact that they trusted me with their secrets, but I never opened up to anyone about the pain I felt. I couldn't tell them that I had just slapped my wife around or about the hate that I harbored for no good reason. But I was an outlet for many people, most of whom I never saw again.

Now that I had a job, I thought that things would just change, and there would be no more fighting, and we could start healing from where we had been. And for a few weeks, it did seem better, but we kept on drinking and partying every weekend, and the arguing kept getting more senseless every time. But that didn't stop us from going out every Friday and Saturday night. The booze and the cigarette smoke were clouding our minds. I never did any kind of drugs, so that wasn't a problem for me. Those are the kind of things that would set me off, and the fights would have been a lot worse than they were.

I can't even remember how we fell into this pit, but I always knew that we couldn't last this way. My fear was that one day I would hit her and really hurt her, or she would finally strike back and do something to me while I was sleeping. Whatever caused us to slip into this cycle of disrespect and loathing for each other was not visible to us because we approached everything with closed eyes and warped minds. To expect that we could live like this was not only stupid but showed a lack of respect for one another. I only speak for myself because I never talked to her about her feelings. I just assumed that her feelings were much deeper than mine. Even with me rationalizing that it was always her fault for getting in my face, it was my responsibility to walk away, or if I didn't walk, there were many things that I could have done to stop the arguing. There is no excuse for hitting her at all, and under no circumstances should you ever let anyone dictate to you how to respond in a negative way to the situation.

My wife was doing everything that she knew how to help with the household expenses. She had gotten a job as a housekeep working in a motel. That work was not what she needed. I tried to convince her that it was better for her to stay home because she was only making five or ten dollars a day. She kept working there for a while and only quit when he tried to make her do more and more rooms for the same pay. Dorothy is not a lazy person, so she would try to get jobs; but because she hadn't finished high school, they were unskilled labor. It drained me to see her trying so hard and not making any headway. I told her that she should just go and finish high school, then maybe she could get a better job. Once she decided to go back to school to complete her diploma, she became a bit more confident in herself.

She went to school until she got her diploma. Now she went looking for a job, eventually ending up at the department of motor vehicles where she worked for thirty years and made a good salary too. Dorothy was a loyal employee and hardly ever missed any days of work, but her workplace was not easy to work in. Many days she would come home from work crying because most of her coworkers had taken the day off. There were some who would come to work and sleep or just not do their jobs, and nothing happened to them. She had too much pride to go there and not do her job. All I could do for her was listen because once you get someone else involved, the trouble begins. She went to one of the upper-level supervisors, and he got them off her back. She would work there thirty years but would never take the promotions that she deserved because if she left her unit, they wouldn't have anyone to get the job done. She is loyal to her friends and places a lot of trust in people that she likes.

Dorothy is what we call a homebody. She likes her house and could be here all day and not go outside. You are always welcome to come here, but it's hard to get her to come to your house. When we stay in a motel or hotel, she would ask the maids to leave the bedding, and she would clean the room. That would make me mad because we're paying them, and she is doing the work. After forty-eight years, she would rather stay at home then to go out to dinner. However, the tide has turned. Since I work from home, it is now hard to get me out of the house. Now I can understand why she was content staying home. You don't have to leave your comfort zone.

I know that she was proud of herself when she got her diploma, but she didn't express the joy that I knew she must have been feeling. After all she spent a lot of time studying, trying to get good grades, she didn't just want to pass her test. She wanted to ace them, and she did very good. It meant a lot to her to finally graduate. It boosted her confidence in herself, but she remained low-key about it. I was so proud of her because I know how much it meant to her. But I was unsure if I could show my glee for her because if I had made a big deal of it, she wouldn't react the way I expected, and I would ruin it for her, so I stayed low-key too. Her graduation went by without any fan fair.

CHAPTER NINE

Self-Awareness

IT IS NOW February 1972. We had been married about one and a half years. I was still on my job and had settled in good. Dorothy has been working at a little motel a couple of blocks away. The extra money she made really helped offset some of the expenses. She would go work there and then come home and cook and clean our house and study. She kept our house clean always. I knew she didn't like working there, but she wanted to be doing something to help with the household income, and she also wanted to have what she called her own money.

Even though things seemed to get better, we still had our fights. For some reason, we could not drink together because it wouldn't be long before an argument broke out. I finally figured it out. It was because whenever she started drinking, she would want to talk about something that I didn't. You talk about personal stuff at home, not sitting in some club or somebody's house during a party. I never told her that, but I knew that was what set me off; and because I got upset, she would want to retaliate, and it would follow us home. We never really would settle anything because after the fight, we never would talk about it.

It's a Friday night in February, and we were at it again. Why? I don't know. Anyway, Tony, her son, was there, and he was really scared and ran next door to get Fred. When Fred came, I was not beating on her. I had just pinned her to the bed so that she would stop hitting me. He pulled me off her and held me on the bed for a while until I cooled down. I was mad that once again, it looked as though I was just beating on her. But it was that night that I thought it was over. I had made up my mind that this was not what I wanted my life to look like.

I had decided that I was going to move out and end all this nonsense. It had really gotten to me. She had gone to work at the motel, so I figured that I would leave before she got home. I was sitting on the bed, crying and thinking, *Why is this happening to me all the time?* I didn't have much to carry, so it wouldn't take too long, but that was the last straw for me. I was not going to spend my life fighting and then worrying about what I had done. The tears were running down my face, and I was in a state of deep depression. I had begun to feel lonely in recent months and had thought about leaving a few months before, but now I couldn't bear it anymore. I had to get out. It did not feel like this relationship would last too long.

I had my face buried in my hands when I felt someone sat down beside me. He was Tony a wonderful child, well-mannered and respectful. He looked at me with sorrow in his face and said, "Pop, are you going to leave us?" I told him that I had to because I was afraid that one of us would get hurt if I stayed here, and I didn't want that to happen. He started crying too and said, "Pop, don't leave us. I love you. Please don't go." I told him that it would be okay, but he wanted my promise that I would stay with them. I said that I would try to make it work, and I would stop drinking so much to see if that would help. That was the day that I decided to change my life. I never told anyone about the talk I had with Tony, and moreover, he had initiated it, but to me that was one of the most moving times of my life. That was the last time I hit my wife. I guess because of what Tony said, I don't know, but I started trying to forget it with no success.

I stayed and started working on myself I didn't stop drinking right away, but I tried to not get drunk every weekend. Tony and I would go for a ride, and I told him that I was going to buy us a house, but he couldn't tell his mother. But she was still drinking, and I would come home from work at one in the morning, and she would have her friend over and would be drunk. However, now I was beginning to understand how I was hurting about everything. The drinking and fighting were all in the front of my mind. My concentration was now on how I could cut down on my habits, not what she was doing. She had never shown any willingness to quit drinking and smoking, and I didn't have the strength or the energy to try and make her stop. I must get right with myself first, and I could see that it was going to take a long time to do it. I would try to set goals for myself, such as, instead of drinking ten beers today, I would only have eight or try to get down to two and a half packs of cigarettes tomorrow. I knew that if I could get started, I would stick to it. When I set a goal, I always did whatever it took to complete it; that's why I would make my goals as realistic as possible. I never made them so hard it was near impossible to obtain them. I always set goals that I know that I can complete, and most of the time I can do more than I set out to do.

Without telling her, Tony and I started looking for a house. I thought that if I showed some interest in making our lives better, it would help us in our healing. We looked at several homes and found one about twenty miles from the city; however, when she saw where it was, she didn't want it because she didn't know how to drive and wanted something in the city. She always used her father to take her places or would catch the city bus. Anyway, that house was out of the question, but now she knew that I was looking for a house and joined us in finding one. We finally bought one in the summer of '72 and moved into our house in June. It was a nice three-bedroom, two-bathroom house with a formal dining room, a large backyard where Tony could play, etc.

Even after we moved, I was still drinking, but I was trying to be aware of when things were starting to go wrong. It is hard to understand because Dorothy wasn't the type of person that would just fly into a rage. Only when we started drinking together was when we could not tolerate each other. But without telling her, I wanted to try and get away from the violent outburst and mental degradation that caused both of us extreme pain. I felt that the responsibility to make our marriage work was mine because whenever I was rational about it, I could tell she was trying to love me from the way she was taking care of me. Whatever she thought I wanted, she would do it.

What I finally figured out was that if I changed, then she would have no reason to fear me because when you get down to it, you understand that her rage was kind of a defense mechanism. Therefore, when she thought that I was about to explode, she would attack first as a way of saying, "I'm not afraid of you." But deep down I came to realize that she was afraid of what I might do. After all, she did know what happened between Charlene and me. I had told her everything that had happened, so in her mind, she probably thought that it could be any day that I snapped and attacked her.

My first and most desperate goal was to stop drinking, and I was working on it. I kept repeating it to myself every day, and as often as I thought about having a drink, I would tell myself why I needed to stop drinking. I would think that if I didn't stop now, I would end up back in jail because I had lost control too many times. If it wasn't with her, it was with a stranger. Everything was annoying to me. I was a lost cause, and I had to make some corrections before it was too late. Another thing I did was to set a date to start my sobriety. It was August 15, 1973. Yep, that was the date that I said I would not take another drink. It was one year from that day that I made the covenant with myself. I told no one about it, and my drinking had curtailed slightly; but that day became my obsession, and that was all I could think about. If I could reach this goal, it would define the rest of my life because if I could convince myself that I can take control over my life again. I would be able to regain the positive attitude that I had before.

Every day when I woke up, I would remind myself of the number of days left, and then I would not be drinking and more. We kept on having parties, but we stopped going to nightclubs, and there were basically the same people always around; most of them were light drinkers. I was drinking less and less because I was really focused on August 15, 1973. That was to be my day of liberation, the day I will remember for the rest of my life. I am feeling good about it because my whole outlook about things was changing. I would not respond so quickly to things that bothered me. I was developing the patience needed to deal with problems. I took notice of the things my wife did to try and make sure that I was happy. I could see more clearly than ever that I was going to meet my goal.

It was Wednesday, August 15, 1973, and the night before I drank two beers. This was way less than I had been drinking a year ago. My day off was Wednesday, so as usual, I went to play golf with a couple friends; and when they pulled the beer out, I said, "No, thanks, I don't drink anymore." That got a big laugh from them, but I drank a Pepsi, and throughout that day I had nothing but soda and water. I hadn't told anyone, so nobody knew what I had accomplished, but I was overjoyed. I didn't have anyone to pat me on my back or to say, "You did it," or "How do you feel?" But I knew that these few hours could not be claimed as a success. I understood that I still had a problem, and the weekend would be my first real test and that this would be an ongoing battle. But to me, I wanted a starting point that was also the end of this part of my life. I made it through that weekend, and my world became so clear. I knew how to stay in control now. I felt so good about things I set a new goal to stop smoking cigarettes two years from the day that I had my last drink. I followed that same routine as I did before. I set August 15, 1975, as the day to stop smoking, and I did. I was smoking two and a half packs of cigarettes every day, and on August 15, 1975, I quit and have never smoked again.

Dorothy said to me one day that she was not going to quit smoking or drinking because she liked it. I said, "That's up to you. I didn't quit so that you could. I did it because I was tired of drinking, and if you want to drink, go ahead." But it wasn't too long after that she did quit drinking and smoking. I don't know why she did it— whether it was because I did or if she just got tired of it as I had. But I was extremely happy for her.

CHAPTER TEN

The Guilt

IT WAS NICE that we were sober now. We would go places and have some fun. Even if there were booze there, I didn't even consider having a drink. I am more than two years sober, and my habits have changed. You see, what I learned from my experience is that if you concentrate on the new habit, the old ones really do fade away. It may have been better if I had professional help, but I did accomplish my goals.

The one thing that haunted me is the fact that I was a wife beater, and as I tried to grow in our marriage, it was always present in my mind. I hadn't hit my wife in more than two years when one day she fixed me breakfast and was sitting there, having a cup of coffee. I thought to myself, here's a woman who does everything for me, cleans the house, washes my clothes, cooks, and doesn't even want my help inside the house. Why did I ever lose my temper with her? How would I ever be able to assure her that I would never do it again? No matter what I say, there is nothing that can give her a complete sense comfort. How can someone feel safe around me, knowing that I had attacked a woman before and knowing that I had done some irreparable damage to her? Who knows if I will fall off the deep end? I know she sees the depression that I feel at times and the impatience that rears itself every now and again.

This had become my bugaboo because when I start thinking about my past and the things that I had done, it is a wonder that she is still here. There are three women that I have laid hands on, which I had considered out of character for me. And no matter how hard I try, there is no explanation for it. I am much bigger and stronger, and they were no match for me. I should have just walked away. All I did was to prove to them that you might be in danger if you push back to hard. I always felt that I was the one who deserved to have the last word.

I used the same logic to approach this problem as I had smoking and drinking, and as for control, I know that I would never strike a woman again. But unlike drinking and smoking, the act of violence lingers in my mind. I can't seem to forgive myself for it. I do now understand much more than I did when I twenty-five years old, and I have learned to let others express themselves, and there is nothing that could make me that angry again. So why do I feel like I am the scum of the earth? Why is it that even though everything my wife does is from her heart, I think she still fears me? And although it's been more than forty-five years since I last hit her, I know that it is on her mind, and she must be wondering too.

I never laid a hand on either one of my sons when they were growing up, but sometimes I feel that they, too, are concerned about how I will react to them. Tony grew up in the house with me, and Ron was with his mother but would come here for the summer and holidays. They are totally opposite each other. Tony will argue all night and was verbally abusive to his wife just to have that last word, and Ron won't put up much of an argument at all. But neither one of them are violent. Tony had a problem with substance abuse (he has been clean for about five years) and has a continuing battle on his hands. Ron drinks occasionally and, as far as I know, has never been in any kind of trouble. They both are good men, but I can sense the worry in their faces and their voices.

The first thing that I do when I get up in the morning is say a prayer, and I always ask God to strengthen me so that I can be of service to someone today and to let me be kind and gentle to every person that I meet. I want to be a beacon of light that one sees when they need someone to listen. I want to be a source to give them hope and a messenger to give them comfort. I know that some people can see in me the answers to many of their problems. I have had people (strangers) knock on the door and ask me to pray with them. A repairman came to fix our refrigerator and told me that when he woke up that morning, he asked God to send him to someone whom he could talk to that day. He said I was his first appointment, and he wanted me to give him counsel. He had just lost someone and couldn't grieve around his family.

I know what is inside of me, and there are times I can express myself, and sometimes the guilt gets the best of me. I fully understand the guilt, and even though I can understand and deal with it, no one knows how I feel because I haven't really told anyone about my feelings. I am still ashamed to tell people that I am an abuser. I am ashamed for hitting the women and because of the lasting trauma that it has caused. While they would be thinking about a big man like me striking a female, I can't forgive myself for the mental anguish that comes with the physical violence. While you see a picture of me kicking and slapping her around, I see more.

I can see the fear in her eyes, I can hear the terror in her voice, and I can feel them weakening while trying to muster up the strength to fight me off. No, you can't image the feeling of having to relive the violent kicking and screaming of someone who is afraid and don't know what will happen to them next, the voice calling repeatedly, "Please don't hurt me." And the whole time you hear and see these horrible things but are in such a rage your whole body is numb to what you're doing. And then suddenly something grabs your attention. It could be a child screaming or a neighbor calling to you, "I called the police," or even your best friend seeing a side of you that no one knew existed. The rage is overwhelming. You have no idea why you did or how it even started, but once you enter that empty zone with no idea of what you're doing, there is nothing to stop you until the victim has succumbed to your relentless attack.

Even when things are great, and there is serenity all around me, I can't help but to wonder how it would be if I had never touched her. Everything is good now, but what would it be like if I had never laid a hand on her? I wonder if she still thinks about the times we fought, or has she put it out of her mind? Has she ever forgiven me, and does she understand how I feel now? My fear is that one day she will remember those days and begin to regret staying with me so long, that she only stayed because she had no place to go. I am waiting to hear that she doesn't love me. How could she after the times I slapped her around?

Sometimes the guilt is unbearable. Fifty-three years after I first hit a woman, and I still can't forget about it. It is as if it was yesterday. In the early days, after I caught my fiancé kissing another man on the doorstep of her cousin's house, I rationalized by telling myself that all she had to do was say that she didn't want me, and I would have just walked away. I could have done that anyway, and I wasn't even sure what they were doing on that doorstep, but now I know that it wouldn't have mattered because it was the rage that took over. The fact that someone would deceive me after me being so good to them is unforgivable to me. No, I wouldn't have walked away; in fact, it would only have enraged me more. The thought that you could do that to me and expect me to just turn and walk away—not a chance.

And Charlene didn't really want to have a birthday dinner for me. She just wanted to have sex with me if she could and was just caught up in the minute when she asked me to come over. I knew this because I had even considered not going to her house because I thought her mother might stop by. Nonetheless, I didn't follow my first thought and went there, and when I saw the guys there, I should have walked away. That self-righteous feeling of, "How could you do this to me, how can you sit there and let this guy treat me that way?" That's when the trouble started. After that, I had the feeling that I never was really in love with her. It was because she was very beautiful and talented. I was mad because she had teamed against me with a man that she had just met in a bar three days before. I also rationalized that because they had teamed up against me that she deserved what she got. I didn't believe that, and no one should deserve being killed because of a relationship gone bad.

I have spent countless hours running it over in my head. What could I do to make up for the mistakes that I made so many years ago? After all, Charlene has gone home to be with her Lord. We did have a chance to talk over the years before her death, and she told me many times that she wished that things were different. She said that she was forced to say that I broke into her house that night and that she shouldn't have taken his side against me. Charlene was one of the smartest people I knew at that time, but she lacked common sense. When the baby soiled his diaper, she would say he just did a little bit so I will change him later and just keep waiting until she thought that he had done enough.

Still my demons were there all the time. It seemed that every minute that I wasn't doing something, I would be thinking about the time I hit them. I only hit Mae and Charlene one time; though it was bad and brutal, it only happened one time with them. My biggest problem of violence was with my wife, the one who has stayed with me for more than forty-eight years; the one who showed her love for me by the way she took care of us and the support that she gives. Through all our problems, she has stayed and endured all the abuse I dished out. She has been the one that is more inspirational to me than any other person. I know it is because of her that I could keep my sanity and work on getting myself better. Though I no longer envision myself hitting a person, I still guard against getting put in a position where I feel that there is no way out.

CHAPTER ELEVEN

Trying to Heal Myself

MY ACTS OF violence have haunted me for many years and have gotten to the point that I couldn't even talk about a man beating his wife or sexually assaulting his teenage daughter. That is the kind of thing that has caused me so much pain. I can only image, if I told them that I physically assaulted my wife, what kind of thoughts would be running through their head. I have also seen other men in similar situations as I am, and I told them that there are no excuses for hitting anyone, and you take a real chance of hurting her bad and spending some time in jail. But I did not tell them that I know from experience what can happen to you because I am an abuser too. I am still afraid of letting anyone know what I'm really like.

Over the years, I was employed by a large company in a position of management as well as owning my own businesses. While still trying to resolve problems in my own mind, I witnessed numerous incidents where families were torn apart by domestic violence issues. I saw how women would deliberately cause problems for their husbands or boyfriends and how men would taunt their wives, trying to put them in a position unfavorable to them. These are vindictive people who were only out for self-gain and didn't care who they hurt if they could get what they wanted. Unfortunately, these are people who garner a lot of attention from the authorities, and many of our decisions are based on the outcome of these kinds of cases.

Domestic violence and child abuse are such widespread problems action is swift and decisive. Anytime you hear about a case, it is dealt with pretty much through the court system. I don't know about a lot of cases, primarily what I see on television or the internet, and those are high profile cases. But those are the cases that I think are resolved and many times does not help in the overall scheme of things. In my opinion, they do little to help solve the problem but add many things to escalate them.

Let me take the case of the football player. I don't know anything about his defense or even if he offered one. I am looking at the news cycle about it and trying to figure out how it helped or hurt abused women. First please understand that I am just a person living with the pain of being an abuser. I offer no professional guidance or advise, just my opinion of why I think the news is awfully disruptive at times. There was a video recording of this football player knocking out his girlfriend on an elevator. It was horrible. I couldn't watch it but one time. Every time a new show would come on, they would show this video. I watch MSNBC most of the time, but there it was, this big football player hitting her and dragging her off the elevator. I would close my eyes. Of course, if you ask the network, they will say that they are just telling the story of domestic violence and how bad it is.

Now you have these women groups calling for the player to be banned from football for life and for the football commissioner to be fired. They are calling on advertisers to stop their commercials and any other support they give the league, and oh yes, the commissioner should donate half of his forty-four-million-dollar annual salary to a charity to help victims of domestic violence. Their campaign is relentless. Somebody should lose their job. The first thing that I heard them say about the victim here was that, when she wanted to accept some responsibility for what happened was, the NFL had brainwashed her. They wouldn't even consider that there could have been an underlying cause that the victim might have been able to help clear up. It was obvious that the victim was an afterthought.

There was no real attempt to help the victim, none that I heard of. It was all about self-promotion, and if they could get some money or get someone fired, they would consider that than helping her. When the victim asked that they not show the video and let them get their life back together, they just kept showing it. So much for supporting the victim.

As I remember it (I don't set in front of the TV all day), they got married, and she was belittled because she wouldn't leave him. If he hit her once, he would do it again. I think that if those so-called help groups really wanted to do something, they should have gotten that couple in for counseling and let them share the blame if that's what they wanted.

Here's what I think and remember. I am an abuser, but I think that when you have someone like me who has knocked women around, you should make sure that this person gets help from somewhere. In my case, I spent time in jail and lost my job. I had no counseling and not very much support in this community because I didn't know anybody. I was afraid and all alone and could have really used someone to help me.

But it doesn't matter how much money you make if you are forced to lose your job. It will not make things better. In many families where there is one breadwinner, we need to find a way to help the family, not to put pressure on them. The fact is, if the welfare of the victim and the abuser were the foremost concern, it would be easier and better to solve the problem. Now, this is a person who makes millions. What about the poor guy who can hardly pay his bills? How does it help to take away his job? And what about the victim? Doesn't it put more pressure on her, knowing that he might blame her for losing his job?

Whether the abuser is rich or poor, there should be a support system that can provide them with counseling before we rush him or her to jail. Common sense will tell you that there are some people who needs to be hauled off the jail right away. However, if there is a way to get them into counseling within hours or a support center, do you think that we could possibly save some relationships? What if there were safe houses where we could send them, could this save the job? I wonder, if I had been able to spend two or three hours talking to someone after I beat up Mae, could they have prevented a second assault? Maybe not, but that would have been the best time to spend with me. After the second time, when I attacked Charlene, I deserved to be put in jail. But if I had gotten some help after the first time, do you think that maybe there wouldn't have been a second time? Cooling-down time will be helpful for some, and there are others who (like me) need to be put in jail right away.

I will keep saying it to my grave, there is never an excuse to hit a woman, but I feel that a woman should bear some of the responsibility to defuse the problem too. I have seen women who knew what would upset their husband and just kept nagging at him. One woman wanted to be with another man, so she enticed her boyfriend into pushing her. She called the police and said he hit her. They arrested him, and she had her way that night. The next day she bailed him out of jail and acted as if nothing had happened.

Now, if they had challenged her too, they could have found a different way to deal with them both. While he did push her (and he shouldn't have done that), the way she was yelling to the police, "He's hitting me," made the situation worse. Let's hear what the victim must say. And before we cause someone to lose their job, let's make sure that they start getting the help they need while waiting for the legal system to run its course. Do we really think that after he or she lose their job, it will make things better? It's easy to say, "Let's get them help," because you don't have a way to be sure that he won't get at her again. What I'm saying is that this is something that we must explore. How can we keep a person out of jail, not knowing if we can control him or her? There is no surefire way to keep them apart without him being under arrest, no safe house where we can be certain that he can't get to her.

I have spent the last forty-nine years trying to understand what went wrong that day I first struck a woman, but the mere thought of the rage—I had blocked any useful reasoning. When I thought that I had killed Charlene, trying to get past that rage was almost useless. Every time I tried to figure it out, I would be blinded by the screaming and the fear in the eyes of the two boys there, watching and begging me to stop. I still have occasional bouts with depression. Whenever I see these violent events shown repeatedly on so many talk shows and newscasts, it makes my blood boil.

But when I wanted to understand the fights that I had with my wife, I could see clearly. There was nothing that should have caused me to react the way I did. With her I could see how much she loved me. I didn't need to hear the words. I could tell because when I woke up in the morning, breakfast was on the table. I had clean house and clean clothes to wear. She always paid attention to what I wanted and never complained about money. She made good with whatever we had. There was no nagging me about this or that. If she could do anything, she would. I could see that she had put all her faith in me. Her very existence was based on what I needed. All I had to do was relax, and none of this would have happened.

After years of battling with what I call personal demons, trying to figure out why I was having such a hard time dealing with my feelings, it started to come together. There were times that I would just go to the park and think for hours. I would force myself to remember things from my childhood. I wanted to go back as far as I possibility could. I had learned a little about self-hypnosis by reading and listening to motivational speakers, so I even tried that too. I don't know what really worked for me, but the more I tried, the more I could understand myself. I could tell that I was making progress because I began to be more deliberate in how I responded to questions and personal challenges. I was more patient and thoughtful about other people's feelings.

Then it hit me. I wanted to show these women how much I loved them and that they could always count on me, but when I thought they didn't accept it, that really hurt me. My feelings were frayed, and I would lose my temper, trying to make them see my love. I needed for someone to let me love them unconditionally and was going to make them accept it. One day I went fishing all by myself. My wife had fixed me some sandwiches and snacks because I was going to do some studying too (I don't think that I bought any fish home more than once). I used this time for reading, thinking, etc. While sitting in my chair on the bank of the river, I opened the cooler that my lunch was in. I started laughing at how she packed everything: bread in one bag, meat in another, condiments in little cups, fruit cut in bite-size pieces, etc. As I sat there, thinking about how thoughtful she was for doing that, it hit me. I think that I know what my problem is. I think I know why I feel rejected, why she couldn't convince me that she was happy with me. That day on the bank of the Sacramento River, I had realized the first step that I needed to take for a better life.

I needed to let her love me and accept her love. She was doing anything that she could to let me know that whatever I needed or whatever I say, she was there backing me up. We are family, and no matter what, she made sure that I was taken care of first. Even if I hit her the night before, when I woke up, breakfast was ready in ten to fifteen minutes. One time I asked her why she cooked for me after a fight. She said, "You still have to eat." You see, these seemingly little gestures don't appear to be significant because they are spread over time, but when you stop and think things over, they become the spirit of the relationship.

These little gestures make you understand that you are not alone. She is always in your corner. These little gestures make you understand that if you can accept her love, then it is much easier for her to express herself. Understanding how and why someone is willing to give themselves unconditionally is a major reason for a faithful partnership. If you can receive my love honestly, then I know that your love will compliment mine. This might sound crazy to you, but if you are having problems in your relationship, spend a couple hours thinking about nothing but your life together. Go back as far as you can and think about those bad days, the times you wanted to leave, the misunderstandings that still exist. Then take a good, hard look at the good times. They may be less, but then look at the quality of those times. Get as many laughs as you can from those times and then repeat those thoughts to yourself. Now all you must do is decide which was better, the bad times or the good times. To me the good times were very precious. They made me happy; and the bad times, well, they were mostly trivial things that should never take that much of my time or energy.

I always said that my love was unconditional, and it hurt me that they couldn't see it. I wanted nothing but the best for them, and they couldn't see that either. They did things to upset me and should have known that I didn't like it. Now I realize that my unconditional love was conditioned on them doing what I wanted them to do. Talking about my situation and following the guidelines that I laid out, that is not unconditional love; it is selfishness at its best. When I realized that I was not allowing them to express their love the way they wanted, it showed me that I needed to do better, not them.

CHAPTER TWELVE

I'm Feeling Better

IT HAS TAKEN me many years of torment and pain to find the answers that would make me feel better about myself. I am much better than I was yesterday, and I will be much better tomorrow and the day after that because I have taught myself how to see the next moment in my day. My willingness to do self-evaluations as often as time will allow is why I can see where a conversation is headed, and once you know the direction, you should be able to cut it off before it gets too hot. Therefore, much of the petty disagreements are either addressed in a reasonable tone and answer or are not worthy of a full-out argument. One way or the other, the stress on the relationship is reduced.

I am still healing, and I have the full understanding that this is a lifetime challenge. There is nothing that I can do to undo the damage that was inflicted in the mind of the people who I bullied. If I could I would take back every slap, every shove, I would. I'd praise them in every way I could. If I could turn back the clock, I would. I would be able to tell Mae that because I was obviously too immature to believe she was lonely as well as I was, I would like to be able to say, "I'm sorry it didn't work out for us. I wish you nothing but happiness."

Healing is looking back at the trouble I had and accessing why I couldn't have just walked away from certain situations. Healing occurs when you can admit that the acts of violence were selfish acts of bullying and not because everybody was taking advantage of you. Selfish acts that caused me to slice the mother of my child, how could I ever tell her how sorry I am? Will telling her I'm sorry remove the scars, or does it remind her of the visible wounds that she sees every time she looks at her hands? If she was alive, she would understand me better today than when she became a friend a few years after our conflict.

Then there are those innocent family members. How do they feel? Will they see a changed man who is extremely sorry for what he did, or have they forgiven me as she had? I don't know how they would feel about me bringing up something that happened forty-five years ago. I have been with them, and we have talked, but never about what I did to their sister or daughter. Her mother, who died some years ago, acted as if she had forgiven me, or at least put it behind her. She never said that she forgave me, and I never asked her for forgiveness, but I think that Margret learned over the years that I wished that I could erase that weekend out of my history.

Healing takes on many avenues of making others comfortable around you. Your actions are always under review. Your voice must be even and not forceful, and questions must not be probing in nature, and answers must be honest and direct. I am now aware of how I sound when I get into a running debate about something. My normally soft-spoken manner becomes a concern to many people. My voice rises slightly and my speech a little quicker, and even though I am not mad or upset, it is perceived that I am. Another sign that I am losing it is, when I do get upset, I use a lot of profanity, something that I don't normally do. These are warning signs to me. If I feel like I'm doing any of these things, I check myself. I know that I will spend the rest of my life fighting my temper and feeling the guilt, but at least now I can control all aspects of my life. I no longer worry about hitting a woman because I know that will never happen again. The consequences of bullying in today's world are unforgiving, and the thought of seeing her face day after day not knowing what's next is unbearable for me.

I still have a great deal of work to do to completely convince myself that I am healing continuously. You see, I must be careful because physical violence is not the worst kind of pain that you can inflict on the ones you love. There is the mental pressure that you inflict on them too. How many times have you said something hurtful to them just to make them mad or bait them into an argument? The screaming, stumping your feet and waving of the hands, the insults are all part of the violent nature that causes the recipient as much pain. I think that this is the worst kind of pressure that you can put on a woman or child. To have them scared every time you open your mouth is nothing more than bullying. And these wounds will linger in their minds forever.

How do you expect to get love or sympathy from them when they don't know if you are going to explode any minute? Why would you want someone afraid of you anyway? Are you that brave that you can harass your mate mentally and then go to sleep while they are in the other room or in bed beside you? Have you ever thought that they might want to end the harassment without regards to what would happen to them? Haven't you seen on television stories about women killing their husbands while they were sleeping? If you haven't, you better start thinking about it. The old tales are true. If you pin an animal in a corner, it will come out fighting; that is true for people too.

We must consider how an eight-year-old or a one-year-old has the capacity to remember those traumatic times in their lives also. I can still hear and see them crying and screaming for me to stop, "Don't hurt my mommy," tugging at my legs and trying to stop me, wondering if they would ever see their mother again. How could I put them through that tragic night in their lives, how could I not think of the two people I loved the most? I don't know if they, don't remember or if they just didn't want to say anything about it. I know that they talk about many things from their early years. Melvin was eight, and he tells me things that he remembers from when we were in Germany. He is such a decent and respectful person. He could be trying to protect my feelings.

Ron was about one and a half at that time, and I can only remember him crying and holding on to my leg. I often think was he trying to stop me or bring me down so that I wouldn't hurt his mother anymore. The memory of them has lingered in my mind for fifty years, and I have never talked to them about it. I see Melvin a couple of times every year, and Ron lives close to me. They treat me with respect, and I still love them both as well as Tony. Tony is Dot's son and has been with me for fifty years. I also put him through the same kind of torment because he saw me and his mother fighting, and he endured the same pain as they did. No matter what they have done or what they have become, it was because they saw in me what they needed in a father, but I was blinded by rage.

I love them, and I need to have the conversation with them about me and my anger. Though I never directed it at them, they received most of it because all they could do was cry and watch the violence.

CHAPTER THIRTEEN

She's My Strength

I HAVE DONE a lot of the things necessary for me to assure myself that I would never hit another woman. The fact that it has already been forty-five years will attest to that. But that is physical abuse. What about the worse kind of abuse, mental abuse? How am I doing with that? I still have a long way to go. It is something that I had not considered a problem for me until I noticed my wife would cut off a conversation when she thought it might get out of hand. That would make me mad, but I would just go watch television or do something else. This is a good sign that I am winning the battle within me. I can just let it go now. Someday I will be able to say that I can train myself how to completely respect any woman or man without ever saying or doing anything that will make them feel uncomfortable around me. I can apologize for my actions and make the case that I am better now.

My strength is in my wife.

My wife has taught me much more than she knows. She is the person who had stood by me through everything that I have done since we got married forty-eight years ago. No matter what it was, she always encouraged me to do what I thought was best. At first, it was hard for me because I wanted her to help make the decision too, so I would be upset that she would say, "If you think it's okay, then it's okay with me." After a while I realized that I wanted someone else to share the blame if things went wrong. But her being there every day made me feel like I could turn the corner and conquer what I now know is a streak of meanness that lies within me. On the outside, I appear to be this soft-spoken God-fearing man, but on the inside, there seemed to be another me who always has evil thoughts and constantly thinking of how to wreak havoc on anyone who crossed me. I have never committed any vengeful acts against anyone. The thought is always in my head. I think it is because when I befriend someone, I do it without any preconceived notions of them being anything but honest and receptive of my friendship. Once you cross me or take advantage of this relationship, it will be hard for me to trust you again, thereby effectively ending the friendship. Oh, I will still treat you respectfully, but can't rekindle what was there before.

With my wife, who was one of the victims of my violent nature, standing by me, it gave me the latitude to do a lot of things without feeling that I was going to hear about it for the next ten years. She didn't know how much this meant to me because I never told her. I would always thank her for things that she did for me, but I never told her how important it was that her encouragement really kept me going. If only I had told her that her thoughts were the fabric that held me together because it gave me strength. When I had a bad day at work, there was only one person who would sit there and listen to me complain without saying a word.

After I had knocked her around in our first couple years of our relationship, she was always there, ready to care for me. I know this because when I need her for anything, she is there. If I am sick, she is the one who makes me go to the doctor and makes sure that I follow the doctor's orders. Until this day she always takes care of me as if I am one of the children and not the one who should be sharing household duties.

I am not so selfish that I think that she has forgotten about the times we had our fights or that she is completely secure in believing that I will never strike her again. She watches those television shows with the wife killing the husband after years of abuse. I don't think that she would harm me, but I know that, watching those shows, she must know how to dispose of me if she wants to. My point is that many women would have left years ago because I found myself yelling at her not too long ago, and she pointed out to me that when I get upset, the yelling starts, and the profanity starts to flow more freely.

We had our fiftieth anniversary a few months ago. I never thought that she would stay with me this long. As I said earlier, she is my doctor, therapist, consultant; whatever I need, she is always there. If it had not been for God placing her in my life, I honestly don't think that I could have made it this far. I don't think that she is afraid of me because she knows how to put me on the right track, and she doesn't back down when she has something to say. I think that she manipulates me to where she wants me to be, but it is usually where I need to be.

Other factors in my healing are from my church family and my brothers and sisters. All my family has been very good to me. I can call any one of them at any time of the day or night, and they will listen. The best thing about my brothers and sisters is that they are not going to let you think that whatever you say will get you sympathy. They will tell you if you are wrong and give you the reasons why you are wrong. I called my older sister a few months before she died because I was feeling that I had a dilemma that was really bothering me, and I had decided and was ready to act on it. She said, "From what you told me, there is nothing to act on because you haven't even tried to solve the problem, so when you talk to the other person, call me back, and then we can talk if you still want to do what you say." I did, and she was right again. It is good to have that support.

Arthur C. Jones Jr., pastor at our church, First Baptist Tabernacle, is a wonderful person too. He is just a few years older than my youngest son. I think of him as family. I can talk to him and come away feeling that I am not being judged but have been told that I need to step back and revisit the problem before making any quick decisions. He is a quiet and unassuming man who always makes the member's welfare a priority. I like his vision and look forward to helping him accomplish his goals. He is a huge part of my support system. His prayers for me and my family mean so much to me.

To have continuous healing, the support system is a must. Those in that support system must be people who you feel will be honest and fair with you. You don't need anyone who will agree with you no matter what. They must be able to tell you if you are wrong and willing to challenge you to meet certain goals or obligations. With a strong support system, you should feel comfortable telling them whatever the problem is and allow them to be direct and honest with you.

CHAPTER FOURTEEN

Confusion!

THERE ARE A lot of well-intentioned groups who are trying to end domestic violence and child abuse, and they are generally doing a good job of it. Many of them are underfunded and depend on donations and volunteers. However, I think that there are some things that unintentionally make matters worse for them. I think that we are so concerned about people like me, the man who they think can't stop and will keep on abusing the victim, we are missing a very important part of the puzzle, and we will never come close to fixing the problem unless we complete the puzzle.

What I am going to say is based only on my opinion and not any studies, facts, or written reports, only my opinion which is based on my experience. I will say what I've heard in news reports, read on the internet, etc. Also, I am not suggesting that anyone is doing something wrong. I just feel as though something is being left out, and some advice given is subjective and may be used for unintended purposes. People are afraid to talk about this for the fear of being called insensitive to the problem. Believe me, I am very sensitive to the problem. I have been haunted by it for more than fifty years, and I am not suggesting that my opinion be used as an excuse but as an avenue to correct the violence.

Here we go!

I have been in positions to deal with the issue of domestic violence in several different ways, and over the years I have watched how a variety of situations has panned out. Again, this is only to show how these situations turned out and not to minimize the seriousness of domestic violence or the methods of treatments used or for any other factual reasons.

Here's an example!

My employer had set up sensitivity-training classes for all the supervisors and managers and then for all employees. My manager was female, and we had a great working relationship. We would tease one another and make comments and jokes (nothing dirty or insensitive or degrading). I would always tell her how good she looked, and she would always grin and say, "Thanks, somebody noticed," so it had been this way for several years until that training class. There was nothing wrong with that training class. It is just what people who walked away thinking that got my attention. The instructor warned us several times through the lecture that everything is not harassment and that we should be sure that before we make a report to evaluate each complaint carefully. She said that we must learn to understand the difference between harassment and a compliment and that it is all right to tell a person that you are offended by what they said and ask them to stop saying it to you.

Five minutes after the class was over, my boss came to my office for our regular meeting. She was wearing a colorful dress, and she looked good as usual. I said, "You look great today. Do you have a date?" I had said that to her hundreds of times, and she always said thanks, and sometime she would comment on my appearance or anything. This time was different. She said I just came from the class and that she might write me up for harassment. I told her that it was the same thing that I always said, and she said, "I didn't know that it was harassment until now." She didn't write me up, but our relationship changed that day; and when I no longer told her how nice she looked, she would ask me, "How do I look today?" I would never answer that question. Here was a situation where we had a good relationship, and no one considered it harassment, but that class put it on the mind of some people that whatever they didn't like was harassment even if that was the first time it happened. I'm talking about women wanting to have men fired because they didn't like the way the men said hello. No one was considering the instructor's saying that a compliment is not harassment, just that they didn't want to hear it from that person.

There a lot of times that I got complaints about my drivers. I was supervising several truck drivers at the time. We were in a temporary office, so the women had to come through our office to get to the restroom. This one young woman would always come through, and if there were drivers there, they would tell her how nice she looked. Her clothes were a lot different from the other women because she always dressed really neatly. So every day she would come through, and the drivers would complement her. I was there, and I heard it every day. She came through one day, and there were seven drivers (including myself) there, and they all said, "Morning, you look nice today." One of them said, "You look very beautiful today!" She turned to me and said that was sexual harassment, and she wanted me to write him up. I was shocked. I heard it all, and because he said the word *beautiful*, it was insulting to her. I told her that we should talk about it before I wrote him up because I could see no intent of harassment and said that I would have to get statements from all those who were there. She agreed, and we went to the conference room and talked. I made her understand that if she wanted him written up, that's what I would do it, but I must find out if there was some underlying reason that I couldn't see that caused her to want him disciplined.

I said, "I see you every day coming through here, and they all complement you. I've heard them tell you in many ways, so why did he bother you? Is there something that I need to know?"

She said, "I just don't like him, and my boss told us that if any of the drivers got on our nerves to have him written up."

I asked her to reconsider because I can't in good faith write him up. I was a witness to what happened, and it would be undermining the spirit of the sexual harassment laws to do it. I assured her that I was not trying to protect him but needed to be honest about her position.

She agreed to just having me to tell him to stay away from her and stop any flirting with her. Of course, her supervisor insisted that I report him, but I couldn't reason with her. She made a big deal out of it, knowing that there were seven witnesses who heard what had transpired. She forced me to file the complaint (with objections), and personnel refused to take any action because he had done nothing.

My point is this. We are so eager to stop the violence and sexual harassment we tell women that it is not their fault; if they don't like it, it is harassment. This I agree that there is never an excuse for a man to harass a woman, and we should preach this using every means of communicating there is. What I need them to know is that when a man uses violence against a woman, if he is like any other abuser, he feels that he has a reason "wrong." Just ask any man or any woman if the hitter gave them a reason or if they thought it was their fault that he or she lost their temper. There is going to be a reason given. No, I will never ever strike a woman again, but there are abusers out there who will take every opportunity beat his woman or children because that is exercising control for him. You can put him in jail, but when he gets out, unless he has some good counseling, he will do it again.

I have read many accounts were a person served time for beating his wife or girlfriend and once released went back to beating on her again. There are at least two people here who need help, and it appears that neither of them got any. Locking these guys up does nothing because chances are that when they are released, they will go right back to the same person. I also feel that she should have the opportunity to seek professional help to guide her through a long process of healing. In my opinion, she feels as guilty, or guiltier than he does, because he has given her an excuse for why he did it (it's usually something she did). Now she must deal with the fact that he is in jail because she feels that it's her fault, and maybe the family suffers, or he loses his job. I haven't done any surveys of thousands of women, but if I talk to ten, their answers are usually the same: "I should or shouldn't have done this or that."

We tell women that it is never their fault, and it is not their fault, but he perceives it to be her fault, and nobody understands him. Most women that I've talked to have as their top priority keeping their family together. They make enormous sacrifices to make it happen. So why don't we, instead of telling them it's not their fault, show them why it is perceived to be their fault, and maybe we can help them avoid the physical abuse that follows a lot of these arguments if she took the position that (and most women know what will set him off) she has some responsibility to defuse this situation. After all, she might spend the rest of her life with this person, and she is not the only person living in a dangerous situation. What about the children? And who are we to tell her, "It's not your fault, so stand there and let him beat the hell out of you," or do we say, "It's okay to humble yourself to him until you can get away,"? Now, I've already told you that I am not a professional consular or psychiatrist. I'm just a person who has been dealing with this personally for fifty years. The torment that continues to haunt me is real, and it takes every bit of my strength, trying to hold back the rage that arises for no good reason. How do we arm her with the necessary skill to maneuver her way through these tense minutes of fear, maybe for her life or the life of her children?

We also put women and men in the unenviable position, being nothing more than chattel to each other. We say that a woman can say no at any time; it doesn't matter how far the act has progressed. In my opinion, this is the most ridiculous thing I have ever heard of. If you could count on everyone to abide by the spirit of this law, it would be perfect, but there are some women who will use it to justify fraudulent claims and everything else. Before these terms came about, I have had women say stop, and when I stopped, they say, "Why did you stop?" The point here is, when you are in the middle of having sex, the man is expected to stop instantly. If he doesn't stop or makes one more move, he can be charged with forcible rape. How in the world is this supposed to stop rape? We need to have more realistic expectations so that we can deal with sexual abuse. Now we all know that men are (in my opinion) far less disciplined than women when it comes to controlling their libido.

The bottom line to me is that we will have a hard time stopping domestic violence and sexual assaults unless we can identify more realistic ways of combating the behavior of both individuals.

Personally, I am very sensitive to a woman's feelings about sexual relationship. If she doesn't want me, then I am fine with that because I need to feel wanted when having sex. There has never in my mind been a reason to force the issue. I couldn't stand someone pretending to be affectionate with me but faking it. But to help prevent him or her from taking a horrible beating, we should tell them that if accepting some of the responsibility will help, if you can't get away from the abuser, have a plan in place, such getting the kids out of danger and a quick exit for yourself. Alert a neighbor to your situation. Let them know that things are getting out of hand so that they might be able to call the police. Running may not help in most situations, but if you can, throw chairs or whatever in his path to delay his chasing you. If possible, unlock the door when he starts arguing so that you can run outside for help. Most of all, if you are aware of his temper and know when he gets to the point of violence and you can't defuse it, don't wait. Leave as soon as you can. He will not be controllable.

It is giving people a false sense of security, telling them that they have no responsibility. I wonder how many people could ward off a fight if they assumed the role of the responsible one. This could also make matters worse if the person feels like he or she is patronizing them. It is a very delicate position, and one must be careful because these people have a lot of rage and are just looking for excuses to attack someone. Your main responsibility is to escape as quickly as you can and not take a beating. Recognize the warning signs, and don't try to be the hero. I know that these things are easy to say, and you might feel that you don't have any place to go, but I think that once you can contact the police, they will have someone for you the reach out to.

I was blessed and able to recognize the rage within me at an early age and could try and control it. As a young man, I was always able to take advantage of favorable conditions in my life. If I did something wrong and got caught but there was no punishment handed down, I wouldn't think, *Hey, I got away with it no whipping.* My mind was telling me never to do that again. I really had a struggle with my temper. It took a lot to get me mad, but when I was mad, it took everything I had in me to settle down. I was constantly afraid that I would hurt someone and end up in prison for the rest of my life.

So I kind of became a loner. I would do things by myself, things like going to lunch or dinner or going to the river and just sitting in my car, watching how people interacted with one another. I had suicidal tendencies. I was always thinking that I would be better off dead, but I never tried or even came close to trying to kill myself. I just kept praying, and sometimes my faith took a vacation; and I would doubt that there is a God because here I am, trying to do the right thing, but he didn't send me the help that I asked for. I quit going to church, but luckily, I didn't regress, and I kept praying and hoping that God would answer my prayer. All I wanted was someone to help me find my way, just to understand me and share the pain, send my angel to guide me through my trouble.

CHAPTER FIFTEEN

My Angel!

SOMETIMES WE ARE so busy with trivial things we overlook the important things in our lives. I had been praying daily, and my prayers were not being answered. There was not even a hint of what I should do. My faith has taken a turn toward doubt, and now my troubles are twofold. On one hand, I am having a terrible time with my emotions, and on the other hand, challenges with my faith. I can't stop thinking about hitting my wife. How could I? She is here every day. I love her, but I wasn't realizing what she really meant to me. I had men who worked for me put in ten-hour days and then had to go home and fix dinner for the kids. If they didn't clean the house, it wouldn't get done.

I would ask them from time to time about being late or taking too long on their route, and they would be honest about what was going on. I had one driver who had a newborn and a part-time job because of the debt he had. He told me that his wife wanted to go out with her friends and that he had to take care of the baby when he went home after his second job. He was always tired and became dangerous to put on the street. If he couldn't drive anymore, then he would have to give up his second job, and that would put him in more trouble with his finances. When he told his wife that he couldn't stay with the baby because he was about to lose his job because he couldn't keep up, she told him that she had a boyfriend and left him.

And second, I had primarily been in and out of the church all my life. My feeling was that I have never asked for anything before, and now that I have, nothing happened. Every once in a while I would say to myself that I was not going to pray today because it feels like I'm begging God to help me, and I don't even go to church anymore. But I would wake up every morning, and the first thing I did was to pray. I always use a simple prayer so that I would always say it no matter what I am doing. I would say, "Lord, I thank you for allowing me to see another day. Father, forgive me for my sins, past and present. Father, all I ask is that you guide my path today. Let me be kind and gentle to every person that I encounter. Bless my family and friends and every person in the world. In Jesus's name, I pray. Amen."

I was a truck driver in those days, and I had gotten hurt on the job and needed surgery on my knee. I put it off for a long time, but the pain became unbearable (and I have a high threshold for pain), so I decided to have the surgery. I went to the hospital and had the surgery. It went well and was successful. But whatever kind of medicine they gave me made me sick. My wife was driving me home from the hospital, and I was throwing up all over everything. I was dizzy and could hardly stand up. She stopped the car and came to my side and cleaned me up the best she could. She would start driving again, and I would get sick again. She stopped and came to my side of the car and cleaned me up. Finally, she got me home, put me in bed, and the next thing I knew, she was waking me up to eat something.

I have never shared this with anyone before. I guess it was my little secret. My wife will find out about it when she reads the book. That day that she bought me home from the hospital was for me the most amazing day of my life. You see, I was sleeping when I heard her voice calling me, saying, "Ron, Ron, Ron, you need to eat something. I fixed you some soup." I thought that I was dreaming at first, but I was wide awake. My eyes must have been closed because she kept calling me. But I could see her just fine. I wondered why she kept calling me. Couldn't she see that I was awake? I didn't believe what I was seeing, and I could not take my eyes off it. When I tried to look away, everything stayed the same, and I was convinced that she thought that I was still sleeping. She had a bright glow all about her. The shining light was very calming to me. As she extended her hand to me, it was like a magnet lifting me up as if I was light as a feather. It was amazing.

That's when I realized it; that's when my world changed. My life had a new beginning. God had answered my prayers because there before me stood my wife. She was in a beautiful light. There was a halo all around her, and everything she said, every time she called my name, it appeared she grew closer and closer to me without moving and inch. God had sent my angel. It had to be her. She was the person who was going to help me get through my trouble, and she was there all the time. I had been given an opportunity to see her with this light all around her. She had to be sent by God, and there is no other way or reason why she would appear to me that way. I thanked God for answering my prayer, and my faith was renewed in him; and from that day forward, I have not lost my faith again. He has answered my prayer long before I knew it. She was always there, taking care of me even when I was mean to her.

My healing started about the time that I realized that my wife was devoting her every free minute to me. I said before how grateful I am to have her. Because of her attention to me, it had helped me to begin to understand myself, and that is why I had the ability to assess myself the way I learned to do it. If only I had known or paid more attention to her, my road traveled would have been much easier and less painful.

You can't forget the fact that I also abused her physically and mentally. But she never wavered with me. She was always there for me. She listened to all my sob stories even when I knew she had her own troubles. I am not naive enough to think that she wasn't having battles with herself. It was her nature to see that I was taken care of and healthy because I was the breadwinner; she thought that even though she worked every day herself. I always knew that I had a great wife. There is no way that I couldn't know that. But I never looked at the possibility that she is the one that God has given me to guide me through the hard times in my life. She has this ability to just sit and listen and not demean whatever it is you want to do; in fact, one of my problems was that she would let me do anything that I thought of as far as business and financing were concerned.

My healing happened because of her and with her help. She made my life more enjoyable. She never put any pressure on me, and she would defuse my rants and not let me get out of hand. Because she chose to be the grownup in the house, I could say whatever silly thing I wanted, and she would say a few things and go to another room. I know that her feelings were hurt many times, and I could tell that she had cried a lot; but she knew that if we got into a big argument, no one knew what would happen.

Because she took the position that many of us won't, she saved my life, and I will always love her because she sacrificed instead of waiting for me to do it. Without her willingness to let me have the upper hand, we have made it forty-eight years. I thank God every day for sending me the angel that I love, and I still pray every day that he strengthens me that I may appreciate the gift that he has given me. She is indeed an angel sent from God to save me from myself. My wife has given me all the strength I need to get through each day, and when I have a weak moment, she is still there to pick me up.

I have spent most of my life in shame about what I had done to those three women. I asked God to cuff my hands that I never hit anyone again man or women. I also pray that every person who is spending precious time trying to eradicate domestic violence and sexual abuse have nothing but success, and I know that they eventually will. I don't know what methods will work or which ones won't. I do know that without them trying, it will continue to escalate, and that is bad news for everyone.

I can only tell you how it has affected me as an abuser for all those years, and no one ever asked me to see a counselor. I was left to conquer my own demons. I was lucky to have someone who felt that I was worth saving, and she did a great job of allowing me to fight my battle, knowing that if I fell, she would be there to pick me up.

I am an abuser. I beat my wife, and I will never be the same.

But I am better today than I was yesterday and will be better tomorrow than I am today!

CHAPTER SIXTEEN

How Did I Get This Far?

I SPEND A lot of time trying to figure out what happened to me and how I got so far off the glory road. How did I become the person I was in my early twenties, the person who dismissed all the things that I was taught? I couldn't image myself being as violent as I was. It was I who people put all their trust; my family, aunts and uncles, and cousins and friends all looked at me as something special. I could do nothing wrong in their sight.

Hank, one of my dearest friends, even though he was several years older, would never dream that I would ever hit a woman. When he found out that I was in trouble, he sent me a letter saying, "This is not your nature, and you will weather the storm because you are in a downfall right now. You need to ask God to see you through." He called me twice a week on Wednesday and Saturday to make sure I was okay, and he would send me money—$10 or $20—once a month; that was a lot of money in 1969. He never let me think that what I did was something that would plague me for the rest of my life. He always said, "You will get through this because you are a good man." Hank died a few years after that, but his interest in me helped rebuild my character.

My brother Raymond also keep me grounded. He would call me and ask if I was working on my temper and to remember that this was not part of my upbringing, and I had to ask for forgiveness. "And God will forgive you, but there is only one person who is going to really set you free. Keep on working at controlling your temper. You are a good man who just had a lapse in your understanding." He reminded me that our mother and father didn't raise any mean children. I could bounce back.

My boss from the phone company also called me several times and talked to me ten to fifteen minutes, but he never asked what I did or why. He would tell me how things were on the job or ask me if I needed anything. I thought that he was calling because I owed him some money for bailing me out of jail that night, but when I had the money to pay him, he said, "You keep it and use it to buy yourself something." I had only known him for a short time, but he had taken a liking in me because of my work ethics, and he figured that I would land on my feet.

Charlene's mother played a great roll in my recovery. After a few years, she would talk to me about things but never said anything about what I had done to her daughter. She was a strong woman and commanded attention wherever and whenever she wanted. I always treated her with respect because she deserved it, and how could I not when I almost murdered her daughter? I wish that I had told her how much it meant to me that she accepted me back in her life. Sometimes I miss her because she was one of those people that you could love one day and hate the next day.

I could go on and on about the people who were there for me: Fred, Jessie, Evelyn, Harvey, and many more. There are some I didn't even know who would just come up to me and say that I look like a good guy and just have a conversation about anything. I now know that God was filling my life with a lot of good people, letting me know that I am all right, and I will make it through my troubled times.

The person that had the most effect on me was a guy that I would sometimes call him Two Letters because his name was JB. JB was my wife's father and one of the best men I had ever met in my life. He would take me for rides in his Chevy pickup truck. Even though he knew that I knocked his daughter around, he let me know that he didn't like it and that one of us might get hurt. JB was a very quiet man who was liked by everybody. To me, he was a father more than a father-in-law. We would ride around for hours, and we would mostly talk about the San Francisco Giants because they were both our favorite team.

He would ask how things were going and would say, "She will be okay. She knows you are a good man." He would always tell me if I needed any money or anything to let him know. I don't remember his drinking or smoking, but he and his wife would come to our house on the weekend, and we would eat chicken wings forever. They were cheap, so we had them at least once a week.

There were three men whom I had the utmost respect for at the time I was so troubled. They were my father, my pastor, and father-in-law. My father was three thousand miles away. He lived in Delaware. He was older and unable to travel, so I only got to talk to him on the phone. He was always worried about me because he didn't want me to leave home and live so far away. He was a great father who lost his wife at age forty-two and raised sixteen children.

My pastor was a very good man who took a liking in me when we joined his church. I liked his vision and dedicated myself to working in the church. He would talk to me and ask how we were doing, but I never told him that I was hitting my wife. He just offered the spiritual presence that calmed me down. Sometimes, when I was having a rough day, somehow, he would sit and talk to me for a long time. Then he would say, "You are God's child. Study the Bible and pray. God has already forgiven you. Now you must forgive yourself. You are here to serve. Fulfill the calling."

My father-in-law was a man of integrity. I never heard him lie to anyone, and he was respectful to everyone. He loved his family and always was available for them whenever they needed him. He would give them anything even when they were taking advantage of him. JB was the most prominent man or person in my life at that time. He was always available if we needed him. He taught me more by not saying a word than anyone. When I left him, I felt like I had renewed my spirit. He was so comforting to be around. The saddest day of my life was when he died. We were on vacation, and he died the day before we got back. I loved him for who he was and the help that I received from him.

It was this kind of involvement that propelled me toward the goal that I had set for myself. You see, I don't need to be in the spotlight or have the attention of everyone in sight. I just want to be able to evaluate myself and the picture around me, being able to rationalize what's before me and understand the exit strategy so that I can correct the problem and move on. However, when you have slapped your wife around, that is not something that you can just move on from. What about her feelings? How have you helped her to deal with the trauma? Does she feel the way that you do? Can she just say, "All right, you hit me, so what?" How can she look at you the same way no matter how great you treat her or whether you tell her that it won't happen again? Have you even talked to her about how she really feels? How many times have you said that you will never hit her again only to fly off the handle as soon as she says something or does something that you don't like?

Can you be sure that you will never do it again? Are you doing anything to ensure that you can cope with whatever comes at you? Who have you talked to about your temper, and did you tell them the whole truth? Maybe you can't afford to see a physiologist, and maybe you can't talk to or don't have a preacher to tell how horrible you are feeling about beating your wife. This is not an option. You must find someone. Even if it's a stranger, talk to them. Show some remorse for what you've done. Be honest with whoever you choose to talk to. Let them weigh in on the truth so that they can give you their honest opinion. Don't mislead them to get the results that favor you.

It was a long time since I had anyone to talk to about my feelings. Fred knew what I had done because he had been there and even pulled me off her a couple of times. About a year ago, a friend of mine also named Ron and I were shopping for a program at church. I also always liked him because he appeared to be a straightforward person. He didn't present a false image. He was trustworthy. That day God put it on my mind to tell him about my life's journey. I am still ashamed about it, but I suddenly had a need to talk to him. I said to him, "I want to tell you something about me because I want you to know." I told him about how I had beat my wife (he loves her; he calls her mother). When I started telling him, I burst into tears. I was crying uncontrollably, and I just couldn't stop. He saw the pain I felt and tried to comfort me. Ron was the only person other than family that I told that to, and once I did, I felt some relief for the first time in fifty years. He knew how hard it was for me, and his reply was, "Thank you, Deak [deacon], for telling me. I can see that it is really bothering you."

When I opened up to Ron, it was another blessing from God. He put him in that car with me because I still needed help dealing with my problems. I know that must be true because when I started talking with Ron, I didn't know that it was still that difficult for me to talk about. Since I've talked to Ron, I have been able to discuss it briefly with another man who told me that he hit his wife for the first time. That was the first time that I didn't cry uncontrollably when speaking about it. My help comes from a variety of places and people. Thank God for putting them in my life.

CHAPTER SEVENTEEN

Always Seeking Relief!

HAVING HAD THE experience of working with other people with problems controlling their emotions, I was being taught a very valuable lesson. As I observed their actions and reactions, I soon picked up on the fact our lives were very similar in many ways.

1. The stories about them working overtime and not having enough money to last two weeks.
2. The wife not working, and the house is always a mess; and if you ask her what she did today, it turned into an argument.
3. She wants to hang out with her single friends until the wee hours of the morning.
4. She never wants to do anything as a family unless her friends are with them.
5. They don't go anywhere or do anything alone; it's like she doesn't want to be with him.
6. There is no affection from her toward him, but any other man gets her attention very quickly.

Because of this interaction by my employer, which allowed me to interview about 130 employees, I soon realized that many of the problems were based on the same premise. I saw that understanding one person gave me the format to help a lot of other people, including myself. I began to relate to these people. Not that we had the same kind of problems. But because their approach was all basically the same, they accepted all the guilt and felt the shame and bore the pain mentally and some physically. I saw the torment they suffered, the agony of constant reminders that they see in other relationships, the kind that they would love to have, and the never-ending responsibility that they feel for their family. You could see their pain longing for some relief, something to help them to find that deep family connection, the kind that recognizes them when they come home after a long hard day of work. Just to have someone welcome you with a warm smile or embracing them with a tight hug—that's not too much to ask of your family when you walk through the door.

It didn't take a long time for me to see some of my problems within these stories. Though my problem was more mental at this point, I could relate to the painful feeling that will eventually show through your action and your conversation and even on your face. I could read those signs in most of the people that came to me because their concerns with the family and marriage were real, and the biting of the nails or the short attention span were telling, but to see the tears flowing down the face of someone hurting and feeling helpless can only make you take notice.

Though it had been many years since I thought that I had control over my temper, I still find myself overwhelmed at times, and I find a quiet place to shed my tears. I would imagine that if I had been talking to someone that I might have cried publicly, but I was not. What I did was painful to me, and to think about it today right now makes me sad, and sometimes I still cry. It is difficult for me to watch people argue because it always reminds me of that period in my life that I do not like to visit.

From these people, I learned that there are more people like me who had done things that we can't undo, and it eats at us continually. The reminders are there wherever you turn. You see someone on television beating his wife; turn to another station, he's trashing his wife, calling her everything under the sun. Still there is no way to avoid the exploiting of women and children through the media. While we know a lot of it is acting, we also know that some of it is real.

I learned that it really takes two people to sustain a relationship and that it can't be one-sided; it must be both parties working on themselves. If only one works on changing their approach to the relationship, then he or she normally becomes perceived as weak, and the conflicts continue to build. Taking the low road is not enough to sustain the relationship because if both don't put something in it, then only one will benefit from it, and that's not solving the problems.

I learned to search my mind for everything thing that relates to my actions, what made me so mad; what caused the rage to build to the point where I was blinded by anything and everything for just a few minutes, and then it all cleared up. I wondered if I had a mental illness or some brain damage. After all, I had taken some blows to the head in my late teens. As far as I can remember, I was a calm, young man, very pleasant and peaceful. I don't recall getting into fights without provocation and not too many then. I didn't ask a doctor if there was anything wrong with me because I always thought that it was self-control that was lacking.

Hearing so many stories and watching the reactions of the people conflicted with their way forward has influenced me. No matter how much I think I have conquered, there are reminders to me that I am still not over the fact that I am a serial abuser. Though I haven't done it in nearly fifty years, I still have thoughts of things that would set me off. I am sure that I will never do it again. My point is that it's a constant battle that lies within me, and my fear is that if I let my guard down just a little bit, I will lose the battle.

I am in the most important fight of my life, and if I lose, it could be very costly to my family. That is why I won't lose. I can't lose because that will mean that for almost fifty years, I have suffered needlessly. My every minute is concentrated on staying focused and keeping my eye on the prize, never repeating the acts of my twenties.

Most of all, I learned that when you listen to other people's problems, they will tell you something about yourself. I learned that I didn't have the nerves to tell my story publicly. I couldn't sit with anyone and spill all the painful feelings that I had. I couldn't tell anyone that I slapped around three women. No, it is too hard for me to let my friends know what kind of person I was. To tell my story would come as a surprise to almost anyone who reads it because that's not what I have projected over the past fifty years. They don't see that in me because I keep it deep inside me, and no one can see it. I don't talk about this because it is too depressing for me, and I try to stay away from things that will cause me grief.

CHAPTER EIGHTEEN

Am I Winning the War?

TO BE ABLE to live a life where I am satisfied with myself will require putting things in perspective. I must understand what it is that I am trying to accomplish and how to accomplish it. As a young salesman, they taught us to set goals and make sure that they are goals that you can achieve. You must lay out a way to reach the goal, and it must have a time to meet your goal. The plan should correlate to the specific goal, with a beginning and an end in sight.

To set a goal to control all aspects of your mind, your thinking, and to be able to measure the success is very difficult. You must feel that you can remember all that you hear or see and then try to bring back everything that you spent years trying to forget. Recalling old memories will also bring back old problems, the ones that you want to stay buried. I need to know how I got to where I was then and where I am now.

I decided to try and recall the painful things that happened to me as a young adult. I would spend at least an hour a day just thinking about my past and remembering all that I could. I am an early bird. I'm always up by four in the morning and try to be at the gym by five thirty. I normally use the room where they hold the training classes because there aren't too many people in that room, maybe two or three. I can ride the spinner for an hour and just think about my life and try to figure out who I am. It helps to be able to bring back memories that you had forgotten. Some good and some bad, but most of the memories I have are good ones. One thing that I discovered is that I have always been timid when it comes to arguing, and because of my quiet demeanor, I lost most arguments. That also kept me out of a lot of arguments too. I wasn't afraid of anything. I just preferred not to engage in a back and forth with anybody; it didn't matter who you were. However, that also led to a few fights because guys would feel like I was dissing them for not joining the discussion.

Another thing that I didn't remember was that I was really a shy, young man. I wouldn't talk to women because I was afraid of being rejected. I thought the best policy was to not say anything in public; that way, no one would hear anything embarrassing that is said to me. As I think back, Mae was the first woman that I approached, and Charlene told me that she wanted me. My wife was as shy as I am. We could sit in the same room for hours and never talk. They became the victims of my violent past. I liked them and wanted them but was scared to talk to them first. Once I knew that they were interested in me, things would be all right. I had plenty to say. I knew how to make them feel comfortable and could keep the conversation going if we were alone. I was never the type that hung out with a bunch of people.

I never had a lot of money. I mean I would work, but I always ended up lending money to people (they never paid me back) to giving it to my sister to help with bills. Money was way back on my list because I could work and make money, so I didn't worry about it. My girlfriends never asked for much. I would buy them stuff, but they never demanded that I give them something that I didn't have. It wasn't a problem with them.

Another fault that I had was that I would not fight to keep a woman. If she wanted to go, then she could go. The truth is that I came to the table, giving all the love I had; and if that was not satisfying, then whatever I did would only prolong the situation. I had a girlfriend who I was ready to ask to marry me, and before I could, she told me that she wanted to separate for a while because she had some deep feeling for this other guy. After the shock wore off, I said fine, and we parted ways. About six months later, she told me that he was married, and they never hooked up.

She said, "I was waiting for you to call, but you didn't, so I'm calling you. Why haven't you called me?"

I said, "You wanted somebody else, so what could I do?"

She said, "You didn't even put up a fight. That means that you didn't want me."

She was right. I never competed for someone's love when I knew that another man was involved.

Being able to spend time trying to recall some important points in my life was quite beneficial because one, I realized that I could remember things that I thought were lost. And two, there were things that helped me put my past in perspective. I found out that I was always a great guy, and I was sure of myself when it came to letting women go without begging them to stay with me. I was also sure that it was not in my nature to slap women around. These things led me to the real problem that I had, which caused me to lash out at them, even if I didn't want them around.

The one constant that was absent in the early days of my adult life was that I was always kind and generous to my girlfriends and never argued with them about anything. I was quiet and unassuming in most respects and was very patient when they wanted to vent or if they had a bad day. My love was always on display for everyone to see. I didn't care who knew it. I would show my love for them everywhere. I smoked cigarettes in those days, but before I went into the Army, I didn't drink booze or anything; but when I came home from basic training, I was drinking, not heavy but enough that I had a drink or two every night. Mostly I would be drinking beer, but occasionally I would drink whiskey, Jack Daniel's, or there was this cheap whiskey, KESSLER'S, and I used to like cold turkey and White Port wine. I remembered that the one constant in those days was that I did not drink a lot. Maybe that's why my temper was so controllable. I wasn't getting drunk and the thought "Treat everybody you meet as if they were honorable" is still intact.

The realization of being in a never-ending battle was one thing that stayed on my mind. I was forever thinking that somehow, I needed to get a hold of myself and get back to the life that I had, the life where I was happy-go-lucky. Nothing seemed to bother me about what other people said or did. I was in my own lane, and only a selected few could enter my space. It was not an option for me to not be friendly and respectful to people; that's the way we were raised. You can let them be who they are. My job is to be nice and selective of those whom I choose to share my friendship.

CHAPTER NINETEEN

Time for Healing!

AFTER ALL THESE years, I still have never told anyone about the turbulence in my life. There are some people who knew the bare basics of my violent past but never any of the constant rage. I have guarded against letting people get too close to me, so I rarely discussed my personal problems with anyone, not even my sisters and brothers. I didn't even tell them that much because they would not allow me to be the victim. If I told one of them that I slapped my wife, I would get the full-throated lecture ("You weren't raised to beat on women"). One of my older brothers said, "It takes a lot of nerves to hit a woman and still go to sleep." He said, "You don't know what she might do to you."

My sister Beck said, "Every time I talk to her, she talks about what a nice guy you are. Is she lying?" Beck told me, "When you were growing up, there is no way that you would ever disrespect any person, especially a woman." She told me to get help with my drinking. "Every time I talk to you, you're drunk or drinking. Do something before you lose the person who loves you the most. If you don't care about yourself, think about her." Beck became the mother of the family after my mother died, so she had put her mark on us. What she said was gospel.

My wife's father had a great influence on my life too. He was not very talkative, and I never heard him raise his voice. I think that he realized that I needed a father figure in my life. He knew that I was beating his daughter but would still treat me as if he wanted me around. Oh, he might say things like, "You two need to stop the fighting because eventually it will come to that point where it never ends." JB (that was his name) wanted the best for his daughter, and he thought that I was good for her.

Most importantly, JB gave me space and would always try to comfort me too. He didn't just come and whisk his daughter away. Now I realize that he would always say, "Let's go get a soda," never "Let's go get a beer." He knew what my problem was long before I did. When I look back over the years, I understand now that he was working on me all along. When I think about it, he was very instrumental in me becoming sober. There are days when I am just sitting, doing nothing, I think of him, and a smile will appear on my face. I thank him all the time for not casting me aside when we were having our problems. I am thankful that I quit drinking and had turned my life around before he passed away. He got to see that what he had done; his subtle manner did work. I loved him as I did my own father, and I miss him as much as I do my father. Anyone who knew him saw a giant of a man always available to help his family and always patient with me.

John Henry, my father, was a very pleasant man. He didn't have a formal education. He told us that he dropped out of school in the second grade to help take care of his family. What he had was an uncanny way of dealing with people on their level. He could talk to you with that warm smile on his face while letting you know that there was a problem, and we go nowhere until it is taken care of. He would take all kinds of insults from people who felt it necessary to embarrass him in front of us. As a teenager, it would bother me that a white man would call him the N word, and my father would just grin and bear it. We would never say anything to Daddy, but we could see how much that hurt him. I would be mad because he didn't deserve that kind of treatment because all he did was speak to a white man.

One day we went to a construction site where my father was working. They were building something in downtown, and he could take us to see the heavy equipment because he knew that we liked it. I don't remember not being proud of my father. I guess that was just a given that you respected your parents and any older person. But there was a white man on the job, and he didn't like the fact that we could be there. He came over to us and lit into us. He was calling us names and using the N word at us, and we hadn't done anything. When my father saw that, he came unglued. He flew into that guy, and it took three men to put him off him. I had no idea that my father was that tough and neither did those guys who rescued their friend. Everybody thought that Daddy was going to get fired, but he didn't. The boss talked to him and the other guy and sent them back to work. I saw them shake hands, but I was scared because in those days, you had no idea of what would happen to our father.

Later, when we were walking home, I asked my father why he did that because people were always calling him names, and he didn't do anything. He told us that it didn't matter what they say to him because he was a grown man, and he had a choice to listen to it or not listen to it. He said that to him they didn't really think of him as the N word; they think that the other white people liked it, but they didn't.

He said, "You are fourteen, and no man should talk to you like that. He can embarrass me, but no one will ever treat my children like that. You can't fight everybody who calls you a name or says something you don't like. I know that when you come to my job, they won't talk to like that again. They know their limit now." All the love that I had for my father was magnified tenfold that day. I could never be prouder of him.

Reaching back in my memory bank, I could recall some moments in my life that really shaped my personality. These are some of the people who showed me what life should be about and that everything is not what it appears to be. To know that I could look back and now understand why JB always wanted to go get a soda. (Because he knew that if he said, "You need to stop drinking so much," it probably wouldn't have worked.) He showed me patience, and he had confidence that he could reach me this way.

My sister knew that I had someone who loved me, and if I didn't straighten up, she would be gone. Beck always liked my wife after she met her the first time. Beck would never take sides either. When my wife called her, she felt comfortable telling her what happened because she knew that I was going to get a good yelling at. The oldest of the girls in our family, Beck demanded and received a lot of respect. She was three thousand miles away but would say, "You don't want me to come to California." I miss her too because she spent her life helping her brothers and sisters.

There are even people who I don't have a very close relationship with whom I will credit with bringing me to where I am. You see, they all had a great deal of confidence in me and trusted that I would read between the lines and find some relief from my problems. I've had strangers take me in when I was stranded, and they were not afraid for me. I've had people come to my door and ask me to pray with them, not knowing at the time that I was seeking solace myself. Because other people see so much in me, I have no choice but to look deep inside myself and find what they see. When I do I think that, I will be more in tune with my own feeling because I don't have a problem showing respect and patience to others.

My healing has taken a step forward because it didn't matter to a lot of people what I was doing; what mattered to them is that they all saw a way out for me. In their own way, each one was telling me that it will be okay, I must work on it. Now that I have a starting point, I can begin to dig deeper in my past to be able to find a solution for the guilt and tearful pain that still resides within me. I still can't erase the images from my mind. I start to shake every time I get upset. I feel weak and afraid whenever I argue with my wife. I am unable to talk for days, and yes, I still hide and shed tears, too ashamed to let her see me crying.

There are times when I am just hanging around, doing nothing, or I might be in a store. Someone will approach me and ask me if I am a preacher. Of course, my answer is no, I'm not. They will say to me, "Do you go to church?" I tell them that I go to First Baptist

Tabernacle Church, and we have a wonderful young pastor. Many of these people have told me, "You have this glow about you, as if you are an angel from heaven." I didn't understand what they were saying until I started really evaluating myself, taking a deep look inside me. It has happened to me so many times that once I looked and bought back the memories, I felt that I do have something to offer. What I have is the truth and honesty, the ability to level with people about questions they have or advice they might ask for.

I will not mislead anyone who ask me for advice or lie to them when answering a question. I am aware of their feelings, and I'm willing not do or say anything to hurt or embarrass them. I will tell them in a gentle and caring manner what I think or feel. I want everyone to know that I will be honest with them because if I'm not, they will find out. When I started evaluating myself, the one thing that helped me dig deeper is the fact that I had people who told me the truth when I asked questions and answered my query for advice with facts or told me that they didn't know how to help me. These are the reasons that I could put my past life to the test and piece together fragments that led to me being successful in remembering the events over the years.

CHAPTER TWENTY

Here's Where I Am Now!

SINCE 1965 I have carried these painful feelings around, wondering if I will ever get over the fact that I am an abuser. Though it has been more that forty-eight years since I've struck a woman, or anybody else for that fact, I am haunted by the memories of the time. I can't remember the last time, but I always see myself striking her. I can see her fighting back, showing no fear. The circumstances escape me probably because the fights were about something stupid. This is not unusual because I couldn't remember the day after it happened why we were fighting, just that it happened. I have been racking my brain for answers with no success.

I am unable to talk to my wife about it because one time we were talking, and she said that I used to beat her up all the time. Not to make a distinction, but that's not the way I remember it. My recollection is that I was trying to fend her off and ended up slapping her around. The way it sounds coming from her is that I was brutal and gave her black eyes and split lips. I honestly don't remember seeing her bruised like that. I can't argue the fact that we fought, and there was so much rage in me I didn't even know where I was for days after it happened.

I want to be able to talk about it to her, but I'm afraid to hear all the things that I must have done. When I talk about the rage within me is because I lost all contact with myself, it was like I had no feeling. I could see no person, no animal, not even myself. The rage took over every part of my being. Nothing seemed to matter. I had no reasoning. I would look in the mirror and see nothing but big, bloodshot eyes staring back at me. I had a fight with this guy one time, and he said that I was so mad he could see death in my eyes. Margret said that when she looked into my eyes, she saw nothing but the devil. I don't feel that I am evil, just that I have a problem with control when I get mad. It takes a lot to get me mad, but when I get mad, no one can reason with me. I'm working on it, have been working on it for many years. I've had some success controlling myself, but is that because I don't join large groups or because I can avoid those situations that causes me to lose it?

I'm at a point in my life where I couldn't put up a good fight. At my age, I shouldn't even be thinking about fighting, but my mentality is to be prepared and fight to the last breath. These are trying times for me, wondering what to do if someone attacked me. How will I manage it if a young man decided to challenge me to a fistfight? Would I walk away, or would I make him beat the hell out me? I truly know that I couldn't match my physical stamina with a much younger man, but my thinking is always, how can I win against him? I plot ways to take him down and, once he's down, show him no mercy, make an example of him. I often wonder if I would kill someone, and the truth is, I feel that I could and would do whatever it takes to protect myself.

During the last fifty-plus years, I have been in this cocoon, trying to stay out of trouble. Not realizing that doing so would create a lot of questions in my mind about where I stand now. Where do I stand as for not backing down from a fight? How would I react to a bully now? In years past, I would never let anyone bully me. Would I really try to beat a person to death, or would I do everything to prevent an argument in the first place? Could I just let someone intimidate me or just take the embarrassment of them berating me?

By these measures, I am uncertain if I have taken complete control over my temper. I couldn't say that I can keep my mouth shut and let somebody intimidate me, especially in front of other people.

I would think that I would end up dead because I gave somebody no choice but to put me down like a mad dog. That's how bad my temper was. Now I think about whether it really matters to me. I mean I keep telling myself that nothing matters to me about what anyone else wants or how they treat me because my goal is to be understanding and try to relieve the pressure of any situation.

Now I am seventy-five years old and feeling like I still have miles to go. I am almost sure that I will never get into another fight, and I am relatively certain that I won't kill anybody. I don't even talk to enough people for them to get me that mad that I would argue with them anyway. I think most people would just ignore me anyway, but that would make me even madder. I have spent many days and nights fighting the anger and evil thoughts, preparing for the time a challenge would come. I feel that I have conquered that part of my physique for several reasons. One, as I said, I am seventy-five years old; two, I am in good shape but still about 265 pounds; and three, I really don't think that I could fight my way out of a wet paper bag. I think that I have complete understanding about my physical abilities.

CHAPTER TWENTY-ONE

What I Did to Gain Control

THERE ARE SOME things that have made me more aware of my anger issues and when I need to check myself. The times when the depression is too great for me to handle or when something or someone gets me upset is when I really need to use any method possible to help me gain control. Most of the time I can relax and get my thoughts in order and concentrate on the positive things going on around me.

The very first thing that I do when I feel boxed in or feel myself losing control, I call on my Father (my paternal father died in 1975). I call on God for comfort. As soon as I sense something coming at me, I say, "Father, take control of my life and bless me with peace and calm through this painful experience." I ask God to guide me through every possible scenario so that I can handle all things put before me and to lead me to an understanding of the person presenting the problem and help me to be patient with them and try to relate to their feelings as well as my own.

Prayer works for me. I don't care what you say, but prayer has bought me through a lot of situations. I've tried many things to calm myself, and they work for a short time; but when I open my mouth and call on Jesus, everything seems to be in my control. When I keep my mind stayed of Jesus, trouble doesn't matter because all my fear is gone. I don't worry about the outcome because it's in God's hands, and once it's in his hands, he will work it out. God is my strength and my salvation. Through him I can do all things.

When I regress, when I am depressed, I try to remember the good times in my life, simple things to remind me of how I would make my wife laugh or how she would cater to me; how or sons would just watch me and start laughing at the way I was doing something. On my good days, I knew that they depended on me to make them forget about their troubles and enjoy a little freedom from the world. We had a lot of fun together, fishing or having picnics in the park and going to the drive-in theater. My wife would make the best hot dogs that we took to the movie. Those were good times.

I still get depressed from time to time, and I cry sometimes even when I'm praying. It doesn't last as long as it did before, but I still have to deal with it. I'm not sure if it will ever go away because even though I pray continually, the devil is still after me. It's difficult for me to watch a man beating a woman on the television or to see them publicly yelling at her or embarrassing her. I can see the fear in a woman in those situations, but mostly they put on a brave front, pretending that they are in control.

I cried a lot. Every once in a while, I would be sitting, watching television, and tears start rolling down my face. I don't want my wife to know that I'm crying, so I try to pretend that my eyes are tired from working on the computer too long. Even when someone has helped a woman or child by doing a good deed, I cry tears of joy. I don't know why I can't shake the depressed feelings or why I relapse so often, but I am feeling better more often than before.

I have been fighting this for so long most of the time I am able recognize when I am in danger of losing my temper. When those times are apparent, I just stop talking and call on Jesus. I say, "Help me, Jesus, take away the pain, take control of my situation, and keep me calm. Father, help me to understand why so much is expected of me, and strengthen me that I might understand all the things required of me to defuse any confrontation." I pray that I can make it through each day without arguing about anything and that I at least try to listen to what is being said to me or about me. If I can turn the problem over to the Lord, I feel that everything will come to a satisfactory conclusion.

I have a hard time saying that I am a Christian because I know that I sin every day. And though I ask for forgiveness and I know that Jesus died for our sins, that my transgressions are already forgiven, I still feel guilty when I pray about them, knowing that I will be guilty of committing sins time after time. But I will always thank God, who sacrificed it all for us. I love the Lord, and I talk to him through his son, Jesus Christ, daily, and I am learning to hear him when he answers my prayer.

Along with my continuous prayer, I spend as much time as I can thinking about what is important to me, what are the things that are dear to me. How will I handle this situation or that program? What if she does this or that? How will I absorb the questioning or show that I am interested in solving whatever dispute concerning the other person? It is very important that you show an interest as to not hurt their feelings, to let them know that you are aware of their problem because it is important to them. Don't be flippant about listening, and try not to say anything that will lead to a worse scenario because it only escalates matters. Whatever the program or complaint is, I try to determine if it is worth an argument. If it's something that I can live with, then I forget about it. If it is serious, then I will deal with it in whichever way possible.

This is a never-ending process, and there are no simple solutions when two people have disagreements. One of the participants must be able to absorb the brunt of the responsibility. I'm not saying that you must say that you're wrong, just that somebody should be able to defuse the tension of the situation. That is a hard call when you're involved in an argument, but if no one takes control of the problem, then it can't get any better. I personally try to just keep my mouth shut. (It doesn't always work, but at least I try.)

My point here is that each individual must consider the consequences of their actions because once you have said something hurtful or lost your temper and became irate about some insignificant problem, there is no way that you can take it back. Oh yeah, they say that you're forgiven, but can you expect anyone to forget how you hurt them? They may not bring it up or talk about it, but it will always be in that memory bank.

For the first time in forty-six years, my wife said to me that she "was always walking around with black eyes." Can you imagine being married and living together all those years and hear her say that? I honestly don't remember things as she does, and I can't say that she's wrong because I do know that I would fly into maddening rages as a young man. What matters is that she sees it that way. I consider her a blessing because of the way she has lived with the same stigma as I have, only she was on the receiving end of the abuse.

My wife could dish it out too. She would drink as much as I did, and we both were as stubborn as a mule. I thought it was all right for me to drink and get drunk, but I also thought that it was not all right for her. I think that I drank a lot more than she did, but we could not drink together. Thank God that she quit drinking shortly after I did. I don't talk to her about it yet, but I wonder if she realizes how much she drank in those days.

Let me be clear so that you understand. I am concentrating on what misdeeds and how I'm trying to deal with them. I think that I am able to force myself to recall many of the problems that I had and many of the things that I've done. I was mostly destructive to myself and my family. I never harmed anyone who hadn't challenged me. I never stole from anyone or was disrespectful to others. I had a sickness, and the only people I hurt were the ones who loved me. I never was physical with my sons. I don't even remember yelling at them, but as I think back over their lives, I can see that I had a negative effect on them. They are fine men with families of their own. My only regret is that I would always tell them to handle their own problems. I thought that because they were adults, they really didn't need my advice. Also, I didn't want to give them advice if they decided that it wasn't what they were looking for and not use it. I didn't know how I would react.

CHAPTER TWENTY-TWO

What Do I Want Now?

AFTER MORE THAN fifty years of carrying this painful information around and not sharing it with anyone, it became apparent that I needed to talk about it. The shame that encompasses me is overwhelming, and it only gets worse. For many years, I wanted to see a therapist but was afraid that the time would be spent on a sofa with them listening to me spill my guts but never telling me what to do. I don't have anything against therapists; they do wonderful work. It's just that I feel like I need more than a few hours a week or a month or whatever I could afford.

While I am suffering within, I got to the point that I am able to see the same kind of rage in other people, men and women and children. I can see that most families who suffer from abusive parents or abusive husbands or abusive wives are very easy to read. I think it's overcompensating affection in public settings or maybe the distant looks in their eyes. I can tell if I am around them on a regular basis. Sometimes they hug each other, but when you look at their posture or their eyes, you see the pretense: kids longing for the real affectionate embrace; a husband afraid to approach his wife for fear of her embarrassing him; or the wife hanging on to the husband, but her eyes are rolling around in her head, wanting to be anywhere but in his arms.

I was born before women's liberation, and since then, there are many movements to bolster women rights. They are certainly right to form self-help groups because they are systematically discriminated against. Women are in the majority now and can change the map on many of the discriminatory practices. The Me Too movement is very engaged now and is making progress toward women's rights. Women are running for congress in much larger numbers and winning than ever before. They are uplifting women and helping them to overcome obstacles preventing them from advancing. They have self-help groups where women can call or go for help when they are in an abusive relationship. I have seen women and children running from a man in fear of being beaten. I have seen women afraid of their husbands and having nowhere to go. These are groups with an understanding and compassion for those who can't help themselves.

I want to see abusive men have an opportunity and a forum where they can learn to express themselves to other men with the same or similar problems. I might be wrong, but I don't know of a hotline where abusive men can call and ask for help. If only we could set up something where they can call and talk to anybody just to calm them down. Maybe they won't use it, but I believe that there are more men out there like me (agonizing for over fifty years with this secret) than those who just want to bully their spouse, their children, or parents.

I want to let other men know that I am a physical abuser who stop hitting my wife fifty years ago but still can't get over it. I wonder how I can overcome what I did. Will I ever be free of the guilt? I search my soul every day when I look at my wife fixing dinner or doing the laundry or cleaning up some mess that I've made. I wonder if she resents me for what I did to her. Does she give it any thought, or does she feel that she bears some of the responsibility? Does she feel that she could have defused an argument? Is that why she acts like nothing ever happened? Or does she really see the good in me?

I want men and women to know that I have spent two-thirds of my life wanting to take back what I did, everything that I had done to her, be it mental or physical, no matter how minor it was or no matter what I thought she had done or how much I thought she was ignoring me. However, I can't. I can only tell you what pain it has caused me over the years. If only I hadn't done it, my live would be much different. I would not be crying about the fact I am an abuser. It is not what should happen when two people love each other.

I want my sons to know how I feel about hitting their mother, that I don't now nor have I ever rejoiced in the fact that did. I can only hope that by them knowing the truth about how I feel, they will understand why I never hit them and why I couldn't face them as the father they thought I was. I live with the shame of being an abuser, and it is very hard for me to get that out of my mind. It is painful and all-encumbering; it consumes me even now. I want my sons to show patience with their family and to know that I love them.

I want abusive people to be treated as sick and to be afforded help as if they had a broken leg. Instead of being sent to jail on the first offense, maybe they can be sent to a home for abusive behavior. I don't want to see families torn apart because he or she loses their job while waiting to go on trial (of course, everyone doesn't fit this profile). We must find solutions that won't put the victims at risk, but we must figure out how to get them in a secure situation and make a judgment on whether they can be put together or separated. As difficult as it is, if they must go in their separate way, try to make sure that their safety has top priority.

I want to share my story, I want to share my feeling, and I want to share how I've been tormented by what I did. I've had the opportunity to work with many different ethnic groups over the years, and I've found that this problem is very serious; and in some cultures, it is accepted if the husband is beating his wife. She has nowhere to go and no one to talk to. I think that by sharing my story, like in many other things, maybe we can have a forum where men will call and ask for help. Maybe they are waiting for somebody to spill their guts and give them the courage to tell about the rage they have.

I want men to step up and really feel the true love a woman has for them and to see the love coming from him. I think that if she sees that you really have remorse for what you did, she can trust you again. For her to see that you are trying to improve yourself might give her comfort that she can feel safe. If you open up and tell your story, maybe she will be happy for you but still want a separation; but because you did open up, you should have better knowledge of how to confront your problems and know that it is not only about you, it's the whole family.

I want to look into his eyes and see past the pretense of a loving family. I want to see that the hugs are believable and that the affection is real. I want the children to look relaxed and not afraid and the wife to have that gleam in her eye as she did before, and I want the husband to show confidence in his family and not look as though he expects things to blow up any minute. You can tell by the laughter or by distant smile. You can see the true love by their reaction to adversity. Is it calm, or is it contentious? You can tell by the mood swings or by the attention span that love did exist at one time, but you see the uncertainty now. You see the wonderment of the fear of making them mad. I want that certainty back. I want to hug you without the fear of being pushed away. I want to be able to tease you without having to explain everything that I do or to see you smile and not look so sad.

I want a forum where men and women can tell the truth about their feelings and be able to listen to other people with the same type of problem. I want them to be honest with themselves and be truthful about their motives and actions, to work on your problem and understand that you need help and gain the confidence to seek professional help. Since men don't feel the need and/or confidence to share their problems with friends or family, they need an anonymous forum so that they can vent their problems.

Men around the world are subject to that type of behavior, and the problem is growing. This is a very serious problem and must be addressed. There are too many of us holding these revelations inside us, and it is tough to keep on hiding it. Now, by revealing my lifelong secrets, I am probably making it easy for people to form a negative opinion of me, but I don't care. I want everyone to know that the pain is unbearable, and it causes me to be depressed even when I see the violence on television. I need to share my story with the expectation that it will help me and hopefully help others.

CHAPTER TWENTY-THREE

Fight for My Sanity!

I DON'T KNOW how to declare victory for where I've come from over the last fifty years. I don't know if I even want to claim victory for being what I should have been anyway. To claim victory seems as though I thought beating on women was some sort of deed required of me or that it was an acceptable practice in which I fulfilled my duty. It would appear as if everyone expected me to abuse my wife and are disappointed that I decided that what I was doing is wrong and against everything that I was taught growing up.

I still have that hollow feeling. It never leaves me. Sometimes I still break down and cry when I think about what I was. I am still searching my mind and soul, trying to figure out why I went through that horrible time in my life. Deep down inside me, I can't recognize that person being there. I can't imagine that I was that withdrawn from reality. To think that I had that much hate and disrespect for anyone who crossed me is unbelievable.

I often think about it now. I wonder, if I had been subjected to counseling back then, would I have been considered insane? I have a very hard time remembering details about that period in my life, but I still picture myself ranting in rage whenever I got upset. I can remember many times that I seemed detached from my body. I would be watching television or listening to the radio, and suddenly it would dawn on me that I had been fighting with my wife just a few hours before and had no memory of it or knew nothing about it except that I did it.

I do recall that in the days when I was drinking heavily, I would black out from time to time. I never told anyone because of the shame I felt. My memory of unsatisfactory events in my life is spotty, but sometimes if I can concentrate enough, I can pull up some things from my past. But this is when the depression sets in, and I can barely think straight. My mind is in overdrive, and all kinds of thoughts encompass me. I really struggle with what is real and what is fantasy. The sad thing is that some things I never know if they are fantasy because they are so bizarre I can't believe that I did them.

My emotions are all over the place, especially when we have had an argument. I lose my temper and yell and cuss a lot when I get mad, but I will isolate myself and try to make some sense of this petty argument. There are times when I am alone that my grief is uncontrollable. I cannot reconcile what has happened. I lose faith in myself and get that empty feeling of abandonment. I have no one to talk to, and if I did have someone, I don't think that I could face what I am. I do call on Jesus to pull me through, and no matter what the problem is or how difficult my understanding is, I gain so sort of control over my emotions.

Of all the things I read and heard, the only one that is constant is when I pray. When I pray, my mind clears up, and I can see things in a better light. While I still can't remember much of what happened, I do feel that everything is going to be fine. I seem to know how to handle the situation better. It might be just going about my business, or it could be going to my room or not saying anything that would add fuel to the fire. When I pray, I'm always afraid that I'm not praying right and feel the guilt of what I had done. I wanted to hear some answers from God. I wanted him to say, "Do this or that," but I never did; but I knew that God was talking to me because my mind cleared up, and I could face what I had done. I did come to understand that God had answered my prayer. I just had to accept what came to my mind and realize that it was his answer.

While I was wondering about my sanity and if I could ever get over what I had done, I regained my faith in God, and I also learned to hear him talking to me. I heard him because that thought about how to defuse the situation didn't come from me. I was too busy feeling sorry for myself to figure out what I needed to do. In the midst of my pity party, it came to me. My mind was free of any other thought. The only thing in my mind was the solution. I would act on that thought without realizing it, and it was better.

God has sustained me all my life, but I would rebuke him because I was afraid that I didn't know how to pray or that I don't read the Bible enough to understand his plan for me. It is extremely difficult to explain at what point that I could hear God talking to me, but the conversation is real though the voice is silent. I still don't think that I know how to pray right or even if there is a right way or wrong way. All I know is when I am in a tough spot, I just say, "Father, I come asking that you remove this troublesome problem. Show me the way. Father, give me the faith to recognize your answer and the wisdom to follow through with the solution. I ask it all in your son, Jesus's, name. Amen." It works for me.

I lean on the Lord for my strength, and I try to witness to others about how he has worked in my life, and he will do the same for others who suffer from the torment that has haunted me for all those years. Even though God has intervened in my life, I still had doubt sometimes, but I know he is always there no matter how much I call on him. Deep down inside, I know how to face my problems, but fear will throw you for a loop. Jesus is there in my heart and soul. That is why I am still here, that is why I still battle the evil thoughts of what I am, and that's why I can share with you this sad chapter in my life.

I feel that God has made it a part of my healing to share my agony and shame with others. I think that he is speaking through me to let others who are suffering with this unbearable quilt that there is help. You are not alone. You must confront your misgivings. I had some powerful men in my life whom I can relate to with how they would deal with similar situations, but I never realized what they were there for. My years of suffering would have been much worse without them; however, I didn't know it at the time. I loved and respected them all and appreciate how they groomed me. I am sorry it took me this long to understand their love for me.

I hope that I never lose my faith again, and it is hard to rely on things not seen, but my experience with God and the results I get when praying are enough for me. If only it was easy to convince people that God will answer their prayer, life would be much simpler. To keep the faith is a chore too. It is very easy to be distracted from what you are doing. Doubt will come at any time, and it will consume you, making you doubt everything you believe; and even if it is staring you right in the face, you deny reality.

Together we must combat the evil forces that keep us from facing the truth about ourselves, that keep us hanging on to the old ways and denying us to see the future. We must keep our eye on what is in front of us and leave the past behind. I feel that I must help pave the way for those who are just experiencing what I've been through. The need to prevent a young man from hitting his girlfriend or wife is my most important job right now. I would hate to see anyone being overwhelmed as I am. I need to tell him that once it happens, you will regret it for a lifetime. You can't take it back. It will always be on your mind. It will go everywhere you go, on her mind and on the mind of every one who knows about it.

Your every thought will be, what are they thinking when they hear us argue? Are they talking behind my back about how I treat her? How does she feel, knowing that all our friends are wondering why she puts up with me? She can have anybody she wants, but she lets me knock her around? What about the young children? Can you see the fear in their eyes when I as much as look at her wrong?

Your children will tell the story without saying a word. All you need to do is look at them, and you can see the hurtful smile, the extra care not to get you upset. Children bear as much pain as you because they walk on pins and needles to keep from setting you off.

I haven't come to peace with it yet, but I am making progress; and I understand that I have a long, long way to go, but I am going to try and understand what God has planned for me. I know that I won't hit anyone again because I have spent fifty years trying to forgive myself. And I still suffer the pain of humiliation every time I see sadness in her face every time I'm watching television and some pimp is mistreating a woman. It is painful for me to talk to my wife about hitting her all those years ago. I can only assume that she could read me and understand me long before I understood myself because she has stuck by my side for almost fifty years.

I'm not as depressed as often as I used to be, but I still have days when I am overwhelmed about my past violence. Some days are unbearable even after all these years. I seem to recover more quickly when I am depressed because now I have learned to hear him when God is directing my path. If I follow what I think are his directions, I am comforted. I try to pray daily, and I always ask for forgiveness for all my sins, past and present. I pray that my wife forgives me as well and that she understands that without her caring during my bad days, I would still be a basket case.

I know that it is hard for men to admit that we have problems; therefore, we don't seek the help that we need. I can't imagine a man hitting a woman the way I did and have seen some men do it with the intent to kill her, not feeling the guilt. If you have hit her and have apologized, then you must be longing for someone to under-stand why you did it. You can play like it doesn't bother you, but we both know that it does. I am glad that I could call on the Lord to strengthen me. I am glad that the Lord put it on my mind what the men in my life showed me. Men that he put there, men who never lectured but just showed me things by doing it—they taught me patience, to respect women and people, and mostly they taught me that accepting God as my Lord and Savior was having faith in things not seen. This taught me how to love the Lord. It showed me that believing in something or someone could shape my life in a positive way.

I am grateful with them, and I thank God, for where I am today is filled with his spirit. I am better today than I was yesterday and will be better tomorrow, and I will be better the day after that. I refuse to revert to violence. I will use every bit of my energy in a positive way. God did it.

CHAPTER TWENTY-FOUR

The Whole Family!

THIS WRITING IS about me and the way I have been struggling with my violent temper and rage for over fifty years. It is sharing with you the difficulty in facing someone that you have mistreated. It is trying to let you know that if it was not for her standing by me, I don't know where I would be now. This writing is trying to tell you that to eliminate domestic violence, we must include the man and the woman in any discussion to change the situation. They both should hear from other people who are dealing with the same problems. No, I'm not saying that it's the woman's fault that she is beaten—that's ridiculous—but we can't just hope that it will correct itself.

I understand that some people will take offense and misunderstand what I'm trying to say. Too many times we just hope things will go away, so we don't say or do anything. We wait for time to pass. But I feel that my problem was that I didn't talk to my wife and let her know my feelings. If I had let her know the rage that I had, just maybe she would have been the one who made me talk about what was tormenting me. She was the one who would eventually change my physically violent nature without knowing it. It was because of her that I stopped drinking, smoking, and fighting. She was the one who would always listen to me venting about my job or whatever. I learned that she is the only person that I could really talk too about anything, but I was too ashamed to tell her that I am sick and need help with my temper.

That's why I think it is very important that we must somehow get people to sit down and be open about what is hurtful to them. I don't care about how other people talk to me because they don't know me; whatever they say I can ignore. But my wife is with me every day, and she knows me, what upsets me and how I respond to certain things. Maybe that's why things that she says are more hurtful. Nevertheless, we should learn how to be open with our partners. If I know something that bothers my wife, I will do my best to avoid doing it. I believe that if I had told my wife about my feelings, she would have helped me get through it many years ago.

There are many self-help groups for women and men today. And though I have never visited any of them, I wonder about how many of them include both sexes. Mostly they specialize in upward mobility and financial equality. I will check to see what is available because I would like to have a blog or podcast or something to generate a real conversation. I think that when a person knows that there are others with similar problems, it will allow them to be more open about their problems.

I believe that a woman with power is just a ruthless as a man with power. Let's not make this about who has the power because it's not about people either feeling disrespected, ignored, or inferior to those partners who just don't know how to respect them or care what they feel. It's about people like me, a loving, caring husband and father but someone who couldn't get past the violent rage that I felt. I was so afraid that I could lose it at any time, so I became withdrawn and kind of a loner. Trying to make you understand the pressure that I would feel to maintain control is too complex to explain, too painful after all these years.

So let the power issue take a step back, and let the relationship take center stage. If we can salvage the relationship and help them find peace, then that's what it's about. This is a family, and every ounce of energy needs to go toward giving them every chance to make it work. But if they don't want to continue in the relationship, let's find out how to help them get through any possibility of violence occurring. It's about people transitioning to a new life and, if there are children involved, a new lifestyle. I have seen many broken families place the children in the position where they must take on the role of the parent.

I am telling you about my difficulty in dealing with the burning desire to overcome my pain and suffering for what I've done. But please don't think that I am not aware of the fact that my wife and sons must feel equally as bad; their anxiety must be higher pitched than mine. They have been very supportive of me over the years, and I love them dearly. If they have any hatred or contempt for me, they don't show it. My wife treats me very good and always worries about me. Sometimes I think that she wants more out of life but settles for what I want. I don't know another woman who would have stayed with me for forty-nine years. I can always count on her no matter what. She is the wife God gave me because he knew that I would need her to keep me grounded.

My sons are two fine men. It doesn't appear that they inherited my temper or are violent in nature. I thank God for that because I did not want to see them be physical with their wives. I wouldn't know how to handle it anyway because I know that they must remember some of the times when I was on the rampage. I don't know at this point if they are mentally abusive or not, but I haven't heard about in recent years. I can only hope that they saw how I was and made the decision that it wasn't the way they would be.

My wife will come under scrutiny simply because she took the abuse and stayed with me anyway. I can hear people talking about her now, how they would never stay with a man who hit them. I see them taking the high road, and many of them will leave right away. But there are others, and the most vocal are likely the ones who are suffering as well. They don't want anyone to know about their problems, so they will magnify another person's plight. There is nothing that you can do about what they say or what they do, but the chances of them being abused in one way or the other are very high.

A few years ago, a gentleman I know was telling me that he had slapped his wife four times in the last couple months. He was remorseful about it but was afraid that she would have him locked up if he did it again. I told him that he should talk to a therapist, and he did. But his wife was telling another young lady who had be beaten up by her boyfriend, "You need to leave him now because he won't stop." Then she went on to say, "If my husband ever hit me, I will be gone in a minute." Therefore, there are a lot of victims who do not tell how they are treated. It might be shame, or they are too embarrassed, or some think that their standing in the community will be jeopardized.

I understand that by writing this book and telling the story of my abusive nature, it puts a target on my back. I fully agree that I should be the last person to believe if a problem arises. I am certain that I will never hit another woman, and I am too old to fight anyone again. So I feel comfortable that any disputes will be settled amicably and without violence. I know that I can lose it at any time, so I must be aware of my reaction to any adversity. 100 percent of my concentration is about controlling my temper. It's about letting them vent and have the last word.

While writing this book, I have discovered a lot of things about myself. Even though I am not completely comfortable looking my wife in the eye and talking about the violence in the early years of our marriage, I am proud that it hasn't happened for forty-seven years. I can also say that I have been good to her and tried to provide a good home for the family. I've tried to show her love and respect and the utmost loyalty. I see her love for me and our sons. She takes care of me like no other woman would. She is the one person who should be put on a pedestal.

I am not a psychiatrist or psychologist. I'm not a marriage counselor. I'm not even sure that I have anything right. I do know how I feel and that there must be other men fighting this same battle, and it is not a pleasant place to be. If you have ever hit your wife or girlfriend or boyfriend or your husband or your mother or father, you must feel ashamed or feel guilty about it because you must have doubts about their feelings for you. If you don't feel any remorse, then you still need help. How can you do that to someone and still expect unconditional love or loyalty? How can you think that you can be mean to someone and fully trust them to not seek revenge?

I never expect to get over the guilty feeling that I have, but I expect to be better than I was yesterday and even better the day after that. I am an abuser and have spent fifty years of my life regretting it. I want to spend the rest of my life recovering from it. I can't change the past, but I can mold the future, and I intend to do my part. I want to talk to any person who has the same demons. I will find a way to do that. I want everyone to listen to other people like them.

CHAPTER TWENTY-FIVE

My Life, My Opinion

THE INFORMATION IN this writing is true to the best of my knowledge. It is my personal encounter with women in my life and the way I treated them as a young man and my battle with depression for the past fifty-five years. It's about what I have personally observed in other people and other cultures. It's about men and women confiding in me, telling me their secrets, not knowing that I was suffering from the same or similar acts and not knowing that I shared their guilt. They were willing to open up to me, but I never revealed my feelings to them. Maybe it was because I wanted them to feeling comfortable around me, or maybe I thought that I would lose creditability with them if they knew that I was in the same boat.

I knew that I helped many of them because I could see their emotions, the way they became productive in their work again, and the many thanks that they gave me. I know that I am not qualified to give people legal advice, and that was not our mandate. Our duty was to listen and recommend professional services to the employees. But there were some people who did not want to go to a psychiatrist or psychologist because they feared that it would create a record that would remain with them their whole life. Those people would just talk to whomever they encountered from the employee help group.

There was one troubled man that I talked to. He was having really bad problems, and it scared me because I could see that he was on the edge. We were not supposed to tell anyone about the people we talked to, and I couldn't report him to management. I could only say that I was recommending him for help. This program sounds as though there were a bunch of amateurs involved who didn't know what they were doing. That's not so. Our job was to listen and direct them to the appropriate professionals for their concerns. That's what I did with this particular gentleman, and he was receiving professional guidance.

One day he didn't show up for work. This was unusual because he always came to work no matter what condition he was in mentally. When I called his wife, a man answered the phone, and I asked to talk to her. She took the phone, and I asked if her husband were home and if he was okay. She said to me that her husband had moved out the day before, and she hadn't heard from him since. She said please not to call her again. When I got back to my office, there was a phone call that he was found dead in his car with what appeared to be a self-inflicted gunshot to the head. It appeared to be a suicide. They said that he had been dead about twenty-four to thirty-six hours. This was a sad time for me because I could see his pain, and there still was not enough time for the psychiatrist to help him.

Because of working in these volunteer situations, I gained a lot of experience reading people when they are troubled. Maybe it's because they mostly pretend that they are happy and have no problems, but if you look deep enough, you might find a very disturbed person crying for help. That's what I see in a lot of men and women living in a violent environment. They tend to wear a false face, but the eyes don't lie. You can see it in their eyes or even the lack of eye contact. Many people will just hope that things will be better if only they can ignore it and not cause an argument. They think, "If I don't say anything, maybe they will forget that they are mad. Maybe it's my fault that they keep getting in trouble at work. If I hadn't been slow in cooking breakfast, he wouldn't be late so much."

It's just my opinion, but I think that the problem for those who will put their job in jeopardy by being late every day is the fault of the person who's late. We can't live inside a person's head, and we can't make their decisions for them nor should we try to take the responsibility for their actions.

I have said before that I have no formal training, but I have been in positions through my employment which required me to pass judgment on people. I refereed sports-making decisions, worked as a supervisor making decisions passing judgments. As a business owner, I made decisions every day whether this was right or that was wrong. Should I fire someone, or how will I handle a certain situation? I am not totally unqualified to analyze a person's habits. I have studied patterns of behavior before, just not in a professional setting. When I say that I'm not qualified, I mean that I am not licensed by any state association, and I don't have a master's or doctorate degree. I can surely tell you how I've learned to subdue my anger over the years.

When I think things over, I remember the difficult times I had just trying to let the thought of hitting these women surface. I would start crying or try to justify it by thinking what they had done to make me hit them. Eventually I learned to allow myself to think about the beatings and the reason, and to my surprise, I did force myself to have a discussion about it. The discussions were one-on-one, the good Ronald and the bad Ronald. At first, I asked myself why, but the answer was always "They did this" or "They did that." Never did the answer include anything about what I did to get them angry. I even tried to rationalize that I was at fault about 20 percent of the time, and they were wrong 80 percent of the time. Even taking to myself, I could find a lot of reasons why I should have just walked away. I needed to find the reason why I didn't walk away.

One day as I was praying, "Eternal Father, I come asking your blessing this morning. I am weak, and I can't do this anymore. Take control of my *life* today and show me how to solve my fear of repeating an act of violence and forgive myself." It was a day later I was watching an old movie on television. I really wasn't paying much attention, and then I heard someone say, "The way you solve problems is to look at the whole scene, then you look at their role and access it, and then you look in the mirror to see the real problem."

The movie I was watching was an old Western, and when I thought about it, those words were not words that should be coming from that movie. I truly felt that God was answering my prayer because I asked him to show me how to solve my problem. That was the day that things changed in my life. All I had to do was to figure out what I was looking for. It didn't take me long to realize that I had to look at myself very carefully to understand it.

I was standing in front of the full-length mirror in our entryway. At that time, it was still hard for me to think about that and not cry, but this time I had a little more control over myself. For a while I couldn't see anything but Mae and that guy standing there, only this time they both saw me and just stared at me. I didn't turn away from the mirror though. I just kept on looking at them, but I got the feeling that something was wrong with me. That thought stayed with me for a long time. It seemed as though, when I was thinking of a different subject, I would feel them looking at me. I knew that there must be a reason for them looking at me when it was her fault. I am the type of person who tries to analyze myself and understand what's happening in my life. After a few days, I understood that I was being told to take a look at myself, that I would find out what my problems are. I would understand after really searching my inner self why I did the things I did, and what they did might have been the best for me. After many days of thinking about it, I figured out how I was going to study myself in order to get the true meaning of what clearly had to be the answer to my prayer. I took about two weeks going over it again and again, and suddenly the thought came to me that I should start over and trace my actions from the beginning. I went back to 1965, the first time I struck a woman. From there I was going to find myself and why I was so violent.

I can remember the first time I struck a woman. The feeling was an angry rage that I had never experienced before. But why did I bother me so much to see her with another man? After all, I had expected that she might not be there when I returned from basic training. Then she had tailed off with writing letters every day, and when I was home on leave, I also always took her home early. If I had not been so ignorant and opened my eyes, I would have had different expectations. I was mature enough to know that there was a chance of either of us wanting to end the relationship. She was eighteen, and I was twenty, and we had to make a decision of magnitude. It was because I was blinded by love for her and my plans for our life. I thought that we had an understanding. Here I am, all these years later, just realizing that she hadn't really agreed to anything, only to talk about.

I discovered that the reason I hit her was not because she was with the guy and not that I was jealous or just couldn't live without her. It was because she had violated my most prized possession—my trust. I now know that I could have walk away, but I wanted teach her a lesson that if you humiliate me, there is a price to pay. So I hit her not because I was jealous but because she dared to have him there and didn't go to see me off. She disrespected me even though she thought that I had left town. I was mad because it was all about me and what I wanted, and I needed that to be known. I tried to rationalize it in many ways and found many reasons why she was at fault for me beating her. But the truth is that even though I always thought about her, I never tried to contact her to ask for forgiveness for what I did, and the one time that I've talked to her since then, neither of us bought it up. I hit her because I lost control of our relationship and didn't know how to accept the fact that she might want someone else. I was being rejected regardless of the plans I had made for us. My feelings were hurt, that's why I hit her, no other reason. While I thought about Mae a lot—she was in the past—her cousin would tell how she was doing. I felt guilty and ashamed to talk to her.

When I met Charlene, it had been about two years since I had seen Mae. I was stationed in Germany, and she liked me from the first time she saw me. We hit it off good while we were there and when I bought her back to the States. She was very smart but lacking some in the common-sense arena. She was also a talented singer. I went wrong with her because she would not stand up to her mother (she would lie to her rather than tell the truth). She lied to her mother about me hitting her when it hadn't happened. I did the best I could as far as supporting the family. I had a good job and income, so we were okay financially. Once again, I trusted that plans we made were agreed to by both of us; however, she decided at the last minute that she didn't want to leave her family and diverted the mover to another location.

The night that I went to jail for attacking her was strange, but it was another night that I could have prevented from happening if only I had not lost my self-control. I went to her house knowing that she was too eager to have me there, but I thought and still think that she wanted me to see my sons. In her mind, she probably thought it would be a good idea to introduce me to her new boyfriend at the same time. But the night went bad when the boyfriend decided that I couldn't touch them. That's when everything got out of control. We were just arguing, and the next thing I know, I was being arrested for just barging into her apartment and starting an argument. From the time that I was put in the police car, my mind was blank, and I could see nothing but anger. The thought of her lying about me starting the argument when she knew it was her boyfriend.

The anger grew to rage, and by the time I got released from jail for disturbing the peace, I grew even worse. If only I didn't have to go back and get my car, things might have been different. I went back to her house to get the car but had left my keys on the table. I knocked on the door and asked her for them, and I saw him, and we started again. Somebody jumped on my back, and the fight started. I was hitting everybody, but all I saw was rage, not people. He had a knife, and I took it from him. I was swinging it at them all. He and his friend ran, and I just kept on stabbing at somebody; it was her. I didn't use the excuse that I didn't know who I was cutting because no one would believe it, but the truth is, when I came to my senses, I was shocked to see what I had done. Having time to think about it, I realized that there was so much rage in me I could have killed her that night. The only thing that I could make any sense of was my son's crying. There were no other sounds—even though she was screaming—that I could hear. It was as if I had been consumed by an unknown power. It was like an out-of-body experience.

Looking still the mirror at who I am helps me to understand why I did it and what the real reason was. Looking in the mirror, I see no one but me because I'm the one who can tell me why I have so much rage and why I was so angry and what I must do to correct what I see. I see a man who tries to own my responsibility. I see a good man feeling misunderstood. I see a man who is extremely sensitive, people close to him not acknowledging his efforts to be a good provider for the family, a good father, a person trying to improve his station in life. The mirror shows me how it was I who was unreasonable, not her. It tells me that I didn't know how to accept her friendship; it says that she cared enough about me to let me know she was moving on.

It was my selfishness that led me to believe she would change her mind and come back to me. Even though she had told me she needed time to think about what she wanted, I knew that she wasn't coming back. I knew that she didn't want to marry me. She didn't have to say it. She showed me. I didn't hit her because of any of those things. It was because she had the nerve to leave me after all that I had done to make us a happy family. I am glad that my answered prayer included looking in the mirror because I have seen a well-intentioned man but also a man where everything centers on him and what he wants, not thinking of what's good for the other people around him. I hit her because she didn't trust me enough to take care of her.

My wife is totally different from the first two. We would drink every weekend, and we would fight every weekend. But when I looked in the mirror, I saw me there with the same problems as before and doing nothing about them. I knew why we would fight and still put us in the position every week. I knew that all I had to do was stop drinking, but I was too stubborn to do that. I was a very heavy drinker in those days, but I still had all rage in the world. When I did get mad, I was unable to control myself. She was just a troubled as I was and drank just as hard. When she wasn't drinking, she was the best friend and woman a man could want.

The fighting with us was normally at home when we both had too much to drink. But even after we had our fights, she would still take care of me. I'd pass out from drinking too much, and when I wake up, she'd say, "I fixed you some dinner. You need to eat something." I wouldn't even say that I was sorry for hitting her, but I was sorry. But every time I did hit her, it really drained me mentally because this was not the way I wanted to live my life. I could tell that she loved me right away by the way she treated me and partially because her cousin told me that he had never seen her this happy before. Still the fighting and the drinking was a heavy weight on my shoulders, and I didn't think I could stand it anymore. As always, especially when I was troubled, I called on the Lord and asked for guidance, and he soon help me to stop drinking. When I was praying for guidance for my marriage forty-seven years ago, God heard me; and shortly thereafter, I quit drinking, and she quit not too long after me. One of the problems was solved, and the fighting would soon follow.

When I think about it, I asked God for guidance in getting my marriage on track. He did not hesitate. We were on the path of mending. And when I prayed for God to take control over my life, he did, and it changed forever. God is my strength and salvation. Whenever I call on him, he is there with the answer. When I asked for peace, he's there. When I ask for strength, he's there. When I asked for someone to love and who would love me, he sent me Dorothy (gift of God). When we were fighting, I would think, *She should stay out of my face, and I wouldn't hit her*. But the truth is, I was afraid of losing her as I did Mae and Charlene. I was pouring out my heart and soul to her, and I couldn't stand the thought of her leaving. When I looked in the mirror, I saw Dorothy too, still standing by my side. Through all the arguments and fights, the ups and downs, there she was after all these years, still worried about me. I am so glad that she stayed with me, and I am so sorry that I ever hit her. It's been forty-eight years now since I hit her, and it will never happen again.

I thank God that he gave me the wisdom to look into that mirror and see myself, a look that even I could see clearly. It made me understand that I am the one who controls my actions, not Mae, not Charlene, and not Dorothy. It's me. I had to live with this guilt for fifty-five years and told no one. I suffered the shame and embarrassment, slightly afraid to let people know who I really am. And one day I opened up to a friend with the same name, Ron, and though I still cry and get choked up when I talk about it, that conversation with Ron is a continuation of my prayer being answered. God has put a lot of good people around me all my life, but I have been reluctant to use their gifts—whether it is someone who just listens or someone to put me in my place.

While I was writing, I just wanted to tell my story because I know that there are millions of men and women who are in the same situation but don't have anyone to talk to. But I say this, if you don't believe in God, then pray to what or who you do believe in. It could be anybody you trust or anything you are comfortable with. It could be the dog, the cat, the car. How about talking to your spouse? It doesn't matter who or what you talk to because the goal is to talk about your inner feeling at length. Try looking in the mirror, and don't lie to who you see. Now I see a lot of different things, but every one of them has meaning and always helps me with my problems.

When you finish looking in the mirror, take a step back and ask yourself, why did it take so long?

SUMMARY

THIS WRITING MAY be meaningless to some people, but to others it might be a release of the demons in their lives. To those in complete control of their circumstances, it might seem silly to think, how could anybody allow something this trivial bother them for fifty years? They may be right that it would be nothing to them, but to me and many people like me, men and women, it is a real struggle to balance the shame of being an abuser and the feeling of, "It happened, so what?" I grew up in the forties and fifties. The only news was basically local. We didn't know much about what was going on outside our town for two or three days, and it didn't linger the next day; it was lost in the middle of the paper. But when a man beat his wife or if the wife beat her husband, it was the talk of the town. Everybody knew it. Even though it was condemned and a disgraceful act, they seemed to take pride in the fact that people knew they fought.

This is a story about me and the things that formed much of my life, about how I was slow to comprehend situations in my life that kept me from advancing mentally as a young man should. When my father hit me with the fire log, I thought about how he felt. I knew he was ashamed of hitting me like that, and he never hit me again. This is about how I always tried to rationalize events in my life; therefore, I came up with reasonable excuses for whatever happened. I was in my thirties before I found out that I was molested, that what she was doing to me was child abuse; and since that topic never came up in conversations and I never told anybody, I allowed it to go on.

I can't speak for others, and I can't even understand why it took me this long to understand my feelings about having beat women. I do know how painful the thought was in my mind. I know that the vision of my rage is scary and is always in my head. In my mind I can still see the fear on their face; that's real, and it has been nearly fifty years since I hit anyone. Every time the thought comes to me, it weakens me mentally because I betrayed everything that I truly believe about not fighting women. Now I can understand the things that would get me upset and have learned to avoid them. I can turn the other cheek and accept what I must do to defuse the problem. I found a release when I told Ron the whole story.

I wrote this book as a way of letting people know what I did and to tell the victims and their families how sorry I am. I wrote it because I needed to share it with someone else who feels the shame and humiliation as I do. I pray that anyone who reads it will be able to learn something about themselves. I think that there are men and women out there in the same position as I am. And I can't imagine anybody hitting another person—man, woman, or child—while feeling the rage that I have and not having any remorse. I want to make people aware that there are a lot of us in the world, and we need to talk about even if it is done anonymously. I want them to know that I haven't hit anyone in nearly fifty years and am just coming to grips with it. I want you to experience the kind of freedom that I am beginning to feel now. I want you to tell me your story so that I can continue learning too. God bless!

ABOUT THE AUTHOR

RON O WAS born in Middletown Delaware but at the age of six-teen moved to Dover to complete his high school education. Ron O always had big dreams, so everyone thought that he would eventually settle in a job that he was suited for. He worked in several different occupations, such as the cucumber factory, the brick plant, or the cold storage. He like driving big rigs and thought that might be for him. The money was good, but he couldn't find steady work driving in Delaware.

Then in 1965 he joined the Army in 1965, where he really grew up. Ron O always talked about writing a book because people would often talk about his creative thinking and storytelling. Ron O felt that *The Agony of the Abuser*, his first book, will impact the lives of many people. Ron O lives in California with his wife of fifty years and has two sons and thirteen grandchildren.

CPSIA information can be obtained
at www.ICGtesting.com
Printed in the USA
LVHW021042030621
689238LV00005B/282